The Athenian Empire

Coinage played a central role
empire of the fifth century BC. I
itself, which was financed th   .... collected
annually from the empire's approximately 200 cities. The empire's
downfall was brought about by the wealth in Persian coinage that
financed its enemies. This book surveys and illustrates with nearly
200 examples the extraordinary variety of silver and gold coinages
that were employed in the history of the period, minted by cities
within the empire and by those cities and rulers that came into
contact with it. It also examines how coins supplement the literary
sources and even attest to developments in the monetary history of
the period that would otherwise be unknown. This is an accessible
introduction both to the history of the Athenian empire and to the
use of coins as evidence.

Lisa Kallet is Cawkwell Fellow in Ancient History at University
College, Oxford. She has published two influential books on
Thucydides, as well as articles on Thucydides, the Athenian empire,
democracy, and Attic epigraphy.

John H. Kroll is Professor Emeritus of Classics at the University of
Texas, Austin, and an Honorary Research Associate of the Heberden
Coin Room at the Ashmolean Museum, Oxford. He is the author of
the volume of the Greek coins from the Agora Excavations and has
written widely on other numismatic topics and on Greek weights and
inscriptions. He has served as Trustee and Second Vice President of
the American Numismatic Society.

Guides to the Coinage of the Ancient World

General Editor
Andrew Meadows, *University of Oxford*

Coinage is a major source of evidence for the study of the ancient world but is often hard for those studying and teaching ancient history to grasp. Each volume in the series provides a concise introduction to the most recent scholarship and ideas for a commonly studied period or area, and suggests ways in which numismatic evidence may contribute to its social, political and economic history. The volumes are richly illustrated, with full explanatory captions, and so can also function as a numismatic sourcebook for the period or area in question.

Titles in the Series

The Athenian Empire: Using Coins as Sources
by Lisa Kallet and John H. Kroll

From Caesar to Augustus (c. 49 BC–AD 14): Using Coins as Sources
by Clare Rowan

The Hellenistic World: Using Coins as Sources
by Peter Thonemann

The Athenian Empire

Using Coins as Sources

LISA KALLET
University of Oxford

JOHN H. KROLL
University of Oxford

CAMBRIDGE
UNIVERSITY PRESS

CAMBRIDGE
UNIVERSITY PRESS

University Printing House, Cambridge CB2 8BS, United Kingdom

One Liberty Plaza, 20th Floor, New York, NY 10006, USA

477 Williamstown Road, Port Melbourne, VIC 3207, Australia

314–321, 3rd Floor, Plot 3, Splendor Forum, Jasola District Centre,
New Delhi – 110025, India

103 Penang Road, #05-06/07, Visioncrest Commercial, Singapore 238467

Cambridge University Press is part of the University of Cambridge.

It furthers the University's mission by disseminating knowledge in the pursuit of
education, learning, and research at the highest international levels of excellence.

www.cambridge.org
Information on this title: www.cambridge.org/9781107015371
DOI: 10.1017/9781139058476

© Cambridge University Press 2020

First published 2020
Reprinted 2021

Printed in Great Britain by Ashford Colour Press Ltd.

A catalogue record for this publication is available from the British Library.

Library of Congress Cataloging-in-Publication Data
Names: Kallet, Lisa, 1956- author. | Kroll, John H, 1938- author.
Title: The Athenian empire : using coins as sources / Lisa Kallet, University of Oxford;
   John H. Kroll, University of Oxford.
Description: New York : Cambridge University Press, 2020. | Series: Guides to the coinage of the
   ancient world | Includes bibliographical references and index.
Identifiers: LCCN 2020009518 (print) | LCCN 2020009519 (ebook) |
   ISBN 9781107015371 (hardback) | ISBN 9781107686700 (paperback) |
   ISBN 9781139058476 (epub)
Subjects: LCSH: Coins, Greek–Greece–Athens–History. | Coinage–Greece–Athens–History. |
   Athens (Greece)–Antiquities. | Greece–History–Athenian supremacy, 479–431 B.C.–Sources. |
   War and society–Greece–Athens–History–To 1500. | War–Economic aspects–Greece–Athens–
   History–To 1500. | Taxation–Greece–Athens–History–To 1500. | Finance, Public–Greece–
   Athens–History–To 1500.
Classification: LCC CJ459.A8 K35 2020 (print) | LCC CJ459.A8 (ebook) | DDC 737.4938/5–dc23
LC record available at https://lccn.loc.gov/2020009518
LC ebook record available at https://lccn.loc.gov/2020009519

ISBN 978-1-107-01537-1 Hardback
ISBN 978-1-107-68670-0 Paperback

Contents

Figures

Maps

Table

Preface

Coinage and the Athenian empire were inextricably linked. It is by no means an exaggeration to say that silver coinage made possible the rise of Athenian sea power and hence the empire itself, constituting rule over more than 200 cities. Since study of the many coinages that lend detail to the history of the empire has been largely limited to specialists in Greek numismatics, our purpose in this book is to make this evidence, much of it involving very recent analyses and discoveries, accessible to students, non-specialists, and scholars of Greek history.

The evidence of coinage is presented in two stages. After an introductory chapter, Chapters 2 and 3 survey the coinages of Athens and of the allied city-states of its empire and discuss how these coinages broadly interacted. Chapters 4–7 are devoted to coinages that add factual detail to the record of particular events, most of them episodes leading up to and during the Peloponnesian War, which ultimately brought the Athenian empire to an end. As Thucydides, the great historian of the war, emphasized, in the final analysis it was a war of competing monetary resources. Coinages of precious metal were at its core.

We have many to thank. Much of this ground was covered some twenty years ago in Thomas Figueira's meticulously researched *The Power of Money: Coinage and Politics in the Athenian Empire*, a work with many observations that largely dovetail with our own. Since its publication in 1998, however, the field has been greatly enriched by new discoveries, particularly with respect to the inscribed fragments and dating of the Athenian Coinage, Weights and Measures Decree, and by the rapidly expanding body of reexamined coinages themselves. Here we owe a profound debt of thanks to Carmen Arnold-Biucchi, Gil Davis, Aneurin Ellis-Evans, Christos Gazolis Jonathan Kagan, Ute Wartenberg Kagan, Andrew Meadows, Selene Psoma, and Kenneth Sheedy for sharing or discussing with us their recent work in published or draft form. Among the many other colleagues who have responded to our inquiries, we thank Peter Thonemann, Alan Walker, and, especially, for unpublished data on coins in the Elmalı hoard in Turkey, Koray Konuk. We are grateful also to the anonymous readers of the Cambridge University Press for their careful reading and recommendations, and to Marcus Chin for compiling the index.

For assistance in obtaining photographs, we warmly thank Peter van Alfen and his colleagues at the American Numismatic Society, Christopher Howgego and Volker Heuchert (Ashmolean Museum, Oxford), Dimitra Tsangari (Alpha Bank, Athens), Bernhard Weisser (Münzkabinett, Berlin), Kay Ehling (Münzsammlung, Munich), Augustinus Zeman (Schottenstift, Vienna), Wolfgang Fischer-Bossert (Vienna), Oğuz Tekin (Antalya), and the auction houses of Lanz Numismatik (Munich), Classical Numismatic Group (Lancaster), Gorny and Mosch (Munich), and Numismatica Ars Classica (London-Zurich).

In keeping with the other titles in this series, the book has been written primarily for university-level students, including those who have no prior knowledge of the Greek language. Appendices explaining coin weights and special terms that are commonly used in the description and study of coins are included. And to assist in locating the dozens upon dozens of place names that inevitably crop up in any political and monetary history of the fifth-century BC Greek world, all places mentioned in the book will be found on the maps in the preliminary pages and Chapters 2 and 6.

Because the size of a silver or gold coin is indicative of its relative monetary value, all coins are illustrated at actual size, even in the case of small coins with inscriptions that are difficult to read. For most of these we have added an enlarged photograph of the inscribed face. Breaks in coin legends are indicated with dashes. Translations of ancient texts, if not attributed, are our own. As for transliterations, we tend to stay close to the Greek but not consistently in the case of proper names that are familiar.

Chronological Table

483   Ship building at Athens

480–479   Persian invasion of Greece and Greek victories in the battles of
Salamis, Plataia, and Mykale

The Pentecontaetia

478	Formation of Athenian alliance (Delian League) against Persia
476	Kimon conquers Eïon at the mouth of the Strymon river in Thrace. It becomes an Athenian colony and *emporion*
c. 470	Failed revolt of Naxos
c. 469	Delian League defeat of the Persian navy at the Eurymedon River
mid-460s	Failed revolt of Thasos
mid-460s–c. 453	Alexander I of Macedon gains control of western Thrace and its mines
457	Subjugation of Aegina
454	Transfer of League treasury from Delos to Athens
447	Failed revolt of Euboean cities
446	Athens and Sparta sign a Thirty Years Peace
441–440	Failed revolt of Samos
	Athenian foundation of Amphipolis in Thrace
435–433	War between Corinth and Corcyra; defensive alliance between Corcyra and Athens; battle of Sybota in which Athens and Corinth come into conflict
432	King Perdikkas of Macedon supports revolts of Olynthos, Poteidaia, and other Chalkidian allies
	Athens begins siege of Poteidaia

The Peloponnesian War

431–421	**The Archidamian War**
431	Sparta declares war and invades Attica
428	Failed revolt of Mytilene
424–422	Spartan general Brasidas invades the Chalkidike, winning over Akanthos, Amphipolis, and other cities
422	The battle for Amphipolis: Spartan victory; Brasidas and Kleon are killed
421	**Peace of Nikias:** treaty and alliance concluded between Athens and Sparta for fifty years
416	Conquest of Melos
415–413	Athenian Expedition to Sicily
413	Spartan fort at Dekeleia in Attica; naval war resumes in the eastern Aegean
413–404	**The Ionian (or Dekeleian) War**
413	Persian satraps begin negotiations with Sparta
412	Revolt of Chios, the first of multiple Ionian defections to the Spartans. Athens makes Samos its naval base in the eastern Aegean
407, 405	Lysander assumes control of the Spartan fleet and receives funding from Cyrus, son of Darius II
405	Destruction of the Athenian fleet at Aigospotamoi
404	Siege and surrender of Athens to Sparta

Abbreviations

Abbreviations of Greek and Latin authors and works follow *The Oxford Classical Dictionary*.

The following special abbreviations are also used:

AIO	*Attic Inscriptions Online*
ANS	The American Numismatic Society, New York
BMC	*British Museum Catalogue of Greek Coins*
CH	*Coin Hoards*. London, 1975–2002 (vols. I–IX); New York, 2010 (vol. X)
IG	*Inscriptiones Graecae*
IGCH	M. Thompson, O. Mørkholm, and C. M. Kraay, *An Inventory of Greek Coin Hoards*. Oxford and New York, 1973
O&R	R. Osborne and P. J. Rhodes, *Greek Historical Inscriptions 478–404 BC*. Oxford, 2017
R&O	P. J. Rhodes and R. Osborne, *Greek Historical Inscriptions 404–323 BC*. Oxford, 2003
SNG	*Sylloge Numorum Graecorum*
TN	J. R. Melville Jones, *Testimonia Numaria, Greek and Latin Texts Concerning Ancient Greek Coinage*, vols. 1 (*Texts*) and 2 (*Addenda and Commentary*). London, 1993, 2007

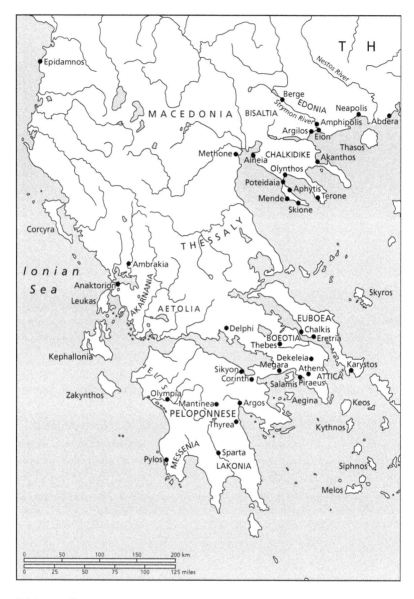

P.1 Aegean Greece

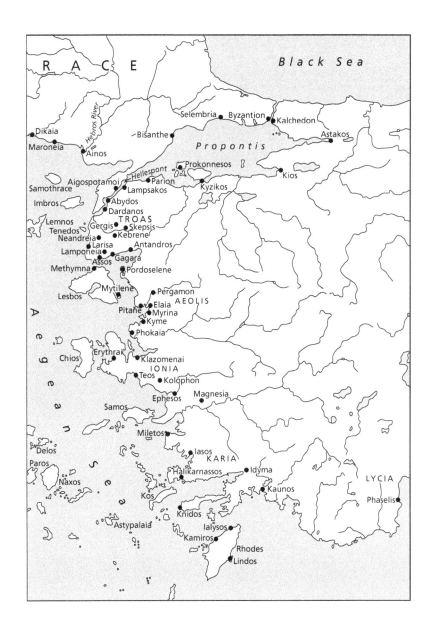

RACE

Black Sea

Hebros River

Dikaia
Maroneia
Ainos

Selembria
Byzantion
Kalchedon
Astakos

Bisanthe

Propontis

Aigospotamoi
Hellespont
Parion
Lampsakos

Prokonnesos
Kyzikos

Kios

Samothrace

Imbros

Abydos
Dardanos
TROAS
Gergis
Skepsis
Kebrene
Antandros

Lemnos
Tenedos
Neandreia
Larisa
Lamponeia
Assos
Gagara
Methymna
Pordoselene
Mytilene

Pergamon

Lesbos
AEOLIS
Elaia
Pitane
Myrina
Kyme
Phokaia

Chios
Erythrai
Klazomenai
IONIA
Teos
Kolophon
Ephesos
Magnesia

Samos

Miletos

Delos
Iasos
KARIA

Paros
Halikarnassos
Idyma

Naxos
Kaunos

LYCIA

Kos
Phaselis

Knidos

Astypalaia
Ialysos

Kamiros
Rhodes
Lindos

Aegean Sea

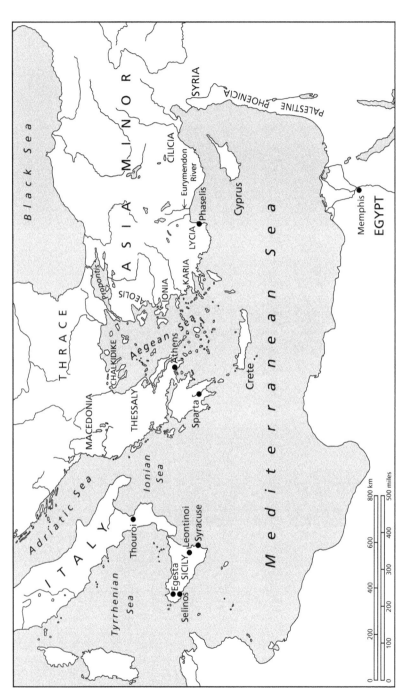

P.2 The Middle and Eastern Mediterranean

1
Introduction

What Was the Athenian *Arche*?

When there were huge surpluses of public funds generated by the mines at Laureion and the Athenians were planning to divide it among themselves at the rate of ten drachmas a man, Themistocles had persuaded them to drop this idea of sharing the money out and to use it instead to build two hundred ships for the war, by which he meant the war against Aegina – a war which, at the time in question, proved to be the salvation of Greece, because it forced the Athenians to turn to the sea. In fact, the ships were not deployed in the war for which they had been built, but they were available at Greece's hour of need. So Athens had already built these ships, and they felt obliged to undertake a further programme of shipbuilding as well. After due consideration, prompted by the oracle, they decided to go along with the god's advice and commit all their personnel to meeting the Persian invasion of Greece at sea, with the assistance of any other Greeks who were prepared to join them. (Herodotos 7.144, trans. Waterfield, adapted)

This passage neatly captures the fundamental link between the abundant wealth in silver that the Athenians had recently recovered from their earth and their rise as a power. That power was explicitly naval, which meant that, unlike land-based powers like Sparta's, it depended on a huge outlay of money for the building and upkeep of ships and pay for the rowers. The combination of money and ships enabled Athens' fleet to be the backbone of the successful resistance to the Persians at sea, most significantly in the battle of Salamis, off the coast of Attica, in 480. This turn of events sets the stage for the history of our subject, which begins immediately after the stunning victories of the Greeks in that year and the next.

The Greeks who defeated the Persian invasion had formed an alliance under Spartan leadership (at that time the preeminent power in the Greek world) conventionally called the Hellenic League. Upon the defeat of the Persians, the alliance remained intact with the objectives of removing them from pockets of territory still under their control and of carrying on a war of liberation of cities of coastal Asia Minor and neighboring islands that the Persians still claimed as their own. But everything soon changed. Owing largely to the outrageous behavior of the Spartan commander, Pausanias, the Athenians successfully contested Sparta's leadership and refashioned the alliance into what modern historians call the Delian League. This was because the meetings of the member states and the League treasury were initially headquartered on the centrally located island of Delos, sacred to Apollo.

The Delian League came into being with Athens as its leader of an alliance, which Thucydides terms a *hegemonia*, that did not impose legal or political authority on its member states. But quickly, as he explains (1.96–99), that alliance transformed into an asymmetrical relationship. In his lexicon of power, the Athenians shed their role as leaders of an alliance of Greeks bound to them in traditional ways in favor of rule *arche* over those Greeks who became subject to them. The translation *arche* as "empire" is not inapposite as long as we recognize that it cannot easily be compared with empires with institutional structures such as formally annexed territories. Athens' "rule" was more informal: while they mapped out tributary districts after some time – initially, Hellespontine, Islands, Thraceward, Ionian, Karian – these were not administrative units such as one finds in the satrapies of the Persian empire, or provinces in the Roman empire, with governors and local apparatuses to facilitate the extraction of resources. Informal, however, does not mean soft power: the heavy-handed encroachment on local autonomy in the cities was seen and felt in many ways, including Athenian officials in residence, the presence of a garrison, and, above all, the obligation to pay tribute.

Herodotos attests to the symbiosis of money and shipbuilding, essential to mobilizing a navy to campaign on an annual basis. Military alliances in the Greek world were no innovation in 478. But those were primarily land-based, involving a hegemon's ability to marshal its allies when necessary, and the allies' recognition that a call-up meant assembling with one's own armor and provisions (and for cavalry, one's own horse). And military alliances were activated in response to a specific, usually temporary, threat. What was unusual – indeed unprecedented – was that the Athenians envisioned a navy that would campaign summer after summer. Because of the expense necessitated by navies, involving outlays for shipbuilding, maintenance, and pay for rowers and other personnel, all of which depended for effectiveness and efficiency on a central coffer, the Delian League required a reliable source of revenue, namely, *phoros*, payable to the Athenians, who provided the financial officers known as the "Treasurers of the Greeks" (*Hellenotamiai*). They were responsible for collecting, administering, and disbursing the tribute.

Initially the term *phoros* was probably innocuous, meaning, literally, a "bringing in," but it became a word with unequivocally negative associations, signifying the subject status of those paying it. "Tribute" is a meaningful translation: the institution of *phoros* evoked Persian practice, in which subjects were obliged to offer annual tribute to the Great King, symbolizing their abject position vis-à-vis the imperial center. Symbolism aside, centralizing sizable monetary resources under Athens' control led to a profoundly unequal power relationship, as well over two hundred city-states, formerly autonomous and free from outside interference, came under Athens' control. No longer was Athens leading free Greek states; rather, Athens was ruling an empire, of which the primary objective was to drain the resources from these cities in order to fund its campaigns.

The necessity of money for a naval empire can hardly be overstressed. Never before in the Greek world had money been the essential factor in the development of polis or supra-polis power. Beginning at the inauguration of Athens' naval *arche* in 478 BC, outlays of centralized, cash expenditures became the norm, demanded not only of the hegemon but also of the Greek cities that signed up, with the exception of several powerful cities and islands (notably Thasos, Naxos, Lesbos, Chios, and Samos) that provided ships and personnel instead of money. Monetary revenue, however, came not just from tribute, whose raison d'être was the funding of the League navy, but also from control of commercial hubs – *emporia* – and custom stations at the Hellespont and the Bosphoros, from which Athens derived income from taxes (when this practice was instituted is not known). In addition, revenue from mining and rents from sacred land belonging to Athena (and possibly a portion paid by cleruchs, Athenian settlers on prime lots of land in subjects' territory) was a key source of Athens' overseas wealth.

While Athens could choose to refer to its relationship with its subjects as an "alliance" (*symmachia*), an explicit example of which are the references to the "allies" and "alliances" in the treaty drawn up between the Athenians and Spartans at the time of the Peace of Nikias (Thuc. 5.18), the unequal relationship becomes transparent. This relationship is manifest from documents not only in which the Athenians made punitive demands on individual cities, or in other cases granted special privileges, but also in decrees that addressed cities throughout the empire as a whole. Accordingly, as in Thucydides (e.g., 2.41.3, 3.10.3–4), we find that in many contexts it is

more meaningful to refer to the tributary members of the *arche* as the
Athenians' "subjects."

Sources

The introduction leads us to the sources for the Athenian empire: How do
we know what we know, and how certain is it? Epigraphic and numismatic
evidence are especially significant.

Inscriptions

Inscribed stone documents concerned with the *arche* are precious evidence, revealing much about the empire, its finances, and the relationship
between Athens and its subject allies otherwise unknown through literary
evidence. Their study is hampered by their frequently fragmentary state
of preservation – many of which had been broken up and reused as
building material; many missing parts mean that a good number cannot
be securely dated.

But we do know that in the year, 454/3, by which point the treasury of
the empire had been transferred to Athens from Delos, the Athenians began
annually to inscribe on marble the portions or quotas of the allies' tribute
that were set apart for Athena and placed in her treasury as dedications.
These were the "first fruits" (*aparchai*) of the tribute, and represented one-
sixtieth of each city's full payment.

The most conspicuous – indeed ostentatious – of these accounts are the
records of the first fifteen years recorded on a gigantic slab (about 1 m wide
and some 3.5 m tall) known as the *Lapis Primus*, the "first stele," set up on
the Athenian Acropolis. The scale of the monument and its contents
endowed it with a potent visual message about who rules the member states
and those states' obligations; no one ascending the Acropolis could fail to be
impressed by this account of subjects' dedications, extracted from the year's
tribute. Critical to this projection of Athens' might were the gods. They
constituted an inextricable part of the fabric and proper functioning of
every polis, and, equally, were central to the existence and well-being of the
arche: the tribute quotas inform us that Athens' Athena had now become
the patron deity of the *arche*. From the subjects' perspective, these monetary
contributions made in the context of a religious observance were a mark of
their submitting not just to Athenians, but to their gods.

Figure 1.1 Fragments of a marble stele inscribed with the tribute quota list from the left side of the Lapis Primus for the year 440/39 BC (*IG* I³ 272). The districts (Hellespont, Thraceward) are listed in large letters with the cities and portions of their tribute (in numbers of drachmas) dedicated to Athena (*aparchai*) following in smaller letters.

As pieced together, the hundreds of fragments constituting the record of cities' dedications provide a wealth of documentary evidence for the organization and financing of the *arche* annually. Each year's entries gives the name and amount paid by each city to the goddess Athena (Fig. 1.1). From these "first fruits" we know that the sums were assessed in talents (6,000 drachmas = 1 talent) of Athenian silver coinage or in fractions of talents: halves, thirds, etc. (see the Table 3.1 on pp. 68–9). By the 450s, most of these assessed sums were probably being paid in Athenian tetradrachms, but we know that not all of them were because a summary at the end of the first year's total informs that part of the grand total included payments in electrum stater coins of Kyzikos (Fig. 3.1), and there are indications in other lists of similar payments in electrum coinages (Figueira 1998, 275–9).

Besides the Athenian tribute quota lists, a remarkable number of other documents pertaining to Athenian financial matters have been preserved in copies that the city had inscribed on stone for public consultation. One

Figure 1.2 Fragment of the marble stele inscribed with the Decree of Kleonymos (O&R 152, *AIO*, probably 426/5 BC). Shown in sculptured relief are containers of tribute money brought to Athens in tied bags and bronze vessels (*hydriai*).

such inscription, dealing with tribute (Fig. 1.2), was crowned by a sculpted relief depicting bags of tribute and the bronze jars which may have carried the money for display at the opening of the spring festival of Dionysos (the Great Dionysia), when the annual tribute was brought to Athens (Lawton 1995, 81; Raubitschek 1941). Although nearly all of these inscriptions survive in fragments, they augment immensely the financial information that Thucydides, Xenophon, and other ancient writers include in their accounts of fifth-century Athens. These literary texts and the surviving inscriptions have traditionally been the two primary sources of evidence for the study of the Athenian *arche*. The coins minted by Athens, its allies, and its opponents, however, make up a third category of contemporaneous evidence. Although on the face of it this numismatic evidence may not seem nearly as informative as Athenian inscriptions, unlike the inscriptions that were produced at the center of the *arche*, the coins were minted and circulated by the separate city-states all around the Aegean and, in addition to their visual and artifactual immediacy, allow a contemporary, broader, and more inclusive awareness of the empire as a whole, while literary evidence, principally, but not only Thucydides, is written with inevitable hindsight.

Coin Hoards and Dies

Before turning to the coinages of the Athenian *arche*, we need to consider two vital kinds of numismatic evidence: hoards and the number of obverse dies employed in the minting of a coinage.

Ancient Greek coins in modern collections exist by the thousands. Although many of these are coins that had been lost in antiquity by accident and have turned up in archaeological excavations or were just picked up from the ground or located with the aid of metal detectors, the overwhelming majority of ancient coins in modern collections comes from hoards, namely, pots or bags full of coins that had been intentionally buried in the ground for safekeeping but because of some unanticipated personal or communal misfortune were not retrieved. Most have been discovered by chance outside of controlled archaeological excavations and were broken up and sold, piece by piece, to supply the insatiable international demand for fine coins by collectors. Nevertheless, many hoards have been saved, or have had their contents recorded for study before being dispersed, and so provide concrete documentation for determining the circulation and chronology of the coins involved.

Of the approximately thirty-six hoards that have been recovered from within the territory of the Athenian *arche* (Appendix B), roughly half consisted exclusively of coins minted by the city in or near where the hoard was found. No surprise: cities minted first and foremost for local use. Predictably as well, most mixed hoards (nos. 27–36) tend to consist of coins from the same geographical region, and these, more often than not (Meadows 2011a, 275–7), are hoards of small fractional denominations of a half-drachma (*c.* 2 g) and less, including tiny divisions of an obol (0.2–0.3 g) that could be accommodated in several different weight systems and were not always easy to distinguish from one another. It is the exceptional hoards, however, that are most informative, like the three hoards of Athenian coins recovered on the island of Euboea (Appendix B, nos. 6–8) that imply that by the second half of the fifth century Athenian coins had replaced locally minted coins at the city of Eretria and probably at the other cities on the island of Euboea as well. Hoards nos. 18 and 19, from Bisanthe and Kios on the Propontis (now known as the Sea of Marmara), indicate that these two cities, which had not yet begun to mint coinages of their own, evidently made up for that lack by employing coinages from other Propontine cities, namely, Parion and Kyzikos.

A find from the Nile delta of Egypt (Fig. 1.3) presents an entirely different kind of hoard, and one that illustrates as well the propensity of economies that produced no coinage of their own to make use of imported coinage. It contained a great mixture of silver coins from all over the Aegean Greek world together with pieces of unminted silver, including several large round ingots of up to 6 cm in diameter. The ingots, and the fact that quite a few of the coins had been test-cut with a chisel to ensure that they were not just silver-plated, reveal that this was not a conventional hoard of circulating coins but a collected mass of miscellaneous silver that

Figure 1.3 Coin hoard recovered in 1901 at Zagazig in the Egyptian Nile Delta (Appendix B, no. 46). Eighteen round, unminted silver ingots and pieces of ingots together with eighty-four coins from two Thracian tribes and twenty-three Greek cities. All of the coins were minted before *c.* 480 BC, except for eighteen Athenian tetradrachms of several styles that date from the 470s into the fourth century BC. Staatliche Museen zu Berlin, Münzkabinett.

could be transacted only by weighing on a balance. Such bullion hoards are typical of silver hoards buried in Egypt and elsewhere in the Near East in the late sixth and early fifth centuries. The present one differs in one important respect. All of the silver was brought together early in the fifth century except for eighteen Athenian tetradrachms of various later styles and dates that were added a few at a time over the rest of the century, except for one that was added still later in the fourth century. As other Egyptian hoards show, this means that while the strong market demand for Greek silver in Egypt indiscriminately accepted imported silver in any form down to the 470s, thereafter the increasing availability of Athenian owl tetradrachms transformed this inflow into a nearly exclusive preference for Athenian coins, ultimately making them a de facto coinage of Egypt.

The significance of hoards extends also to the absolute dating of Greek coinages. Inasmuch as nearly all Greek civic coins were designed and minted without any inscribed indication of date, in assigning dates to coinages, scholars have had to rely on educated guesswork from whatever stylistic or other criteria might be relevant, including probable historical contexts, and, in the case of coins recovered in controlled excavations, from their archaeological contexts. Besides being a source of most new coins, hoards provide chronological evidence of a uniquely comparative kind since in any assemblage of mixed coinages, the most credibly dated later specimens serve as chronological pegs for adjusting the chronology of the less well dated coins buried with them.

The spectacular hoard of more than 1,900 Greek silver coins found by villagers in 1984 in the town of Emalı in the Lycian uplands of south-western Turkey (Map 2.2) illustrates how a newly discovered hoard can correct previously accepted chronologies (Appendix B, no. 41; Fried 1987; Kagan 1987). Now largely housed in the archaeological museum in the Turkish city of Antalya, the hoard was originally referred to as the "Dec-adrachm Hoard" because of the most stunning coins in it: thirteen large Athenian decadrachms, like the one illustrated in Fig. 2.5. Altogether, the hoard contained coins from twenty-two cities of Aegean Greece and seven Thracian tribes together with nearly a thousand coins of local Lycian rulers in the general region where it was found.

A number of the latest reliably dated coins in the hoard, like those of Athens in Fig. 2.4 and others from Samos, indicate a burial date of around 460 BC or slightly before. Accordingly, to take just two instances, the latest specimens of two major civic coinages of Northern Greece that are well represented in the hoard, the coinages of Akanthos and Abdera, are shown to belong to the 460s (and not the 480s or 470s, as these coins had been dated previously), a chronological shift of ten to twenty years that significantly lowers the dating of the cities' subsequent coinages in the second half of the fifth century as well (cf. Figs. 3.9b and 3.15a). Likewise, the coins of the Thracian tribe of the Bisalti (Fig. 4.5), which do not appear in hoards earlier than the Elmalı hoard, must date not, as formerly believed, to the decades before 480 BC when Thrace was under Persian rule, but rather began in the 470s, after the Persians had departed. In other cases, the hoard has served to reinforce the correctness of existing chronologies.

Historical information of another kind from the Emalı find concerns the volume of silver coinage that was being produced in two major mining regions during the 70s and 60s of the fifth century. One of these was the

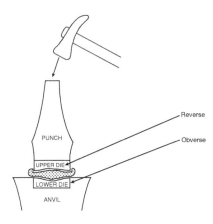

Figure 1.4 The striking of ancient coins. Engraved dies for the striking of coins were normally made of hardened bronze. This diagram shows why the minting of a coinage tended to employ more reverse (or punch) dies than obverse (or anvil) dies. Because the punch dies received the full force of the striking hammer, they were liable to break or develop cracks sooner than the obverse dies that were somewhat cushioned from the blow of the hammer by the silver or gold blank on top and were also supported by the mass of the anvil into which they were inserted.

Thracian region of Bisaltia on the western bank of the Strymon River where the aforementioned tribal coins were produced. These large, showy coins (Fig. 4.5), weighing about 29 g each, were relatively rare until their numbers were suddenly boosted by the sixty-eight specimens in the Emalı hoard. These, moreover, had been stamped out from some twenty-six obverse and forty-five reverse dies. As shown in Fig. 1.4, the stamping of ancient coins was done manually, and since the coin designs were engraved in sunken relief into the faces of the hard metal dies also by hand, no two obverse or reverse dies are exactly alike. Since it is estimated that one obverse coin die could have served to strike on average up to about 20,000 silver coins (de Callataÿ 2011), the original number of coins represented by these twenty-six dies would have come to over half a million – if all of the dies were used until they broke or wore out. Dies for such exceptionally big coins probably did not have such a lengthy working life expectancy. Yet when one makes allowance for additional obverse dies that were not represented in the Emalı sample but can be roughly estimated through formulas of statistical probability, the estimated volume of the Bisaltian coinage remains huge. For a coinage of such large pieces that was minted within a space of only about ten to fifteen years, even the most conservative projection reveals how extraordinary the deposit or deposits of silver under the control of this single Thracian tribe must have been. (Indeed, the scale of the Bisalti coinage was greater than the Emalı sample allows, as the Carchemish hoard of 1996 (Appendix B, no. 44), adds additional obverse dies from a continuation of the coinage after *c.* 460).

That coinage, however, was not nearly as prolific as the coinage being minted by the city of Athens from silver extracted from its mines in southeast Attica. Although the phases of this coinage from the end of the

Persian Wars in 479 to the *c.* 460 BC time of the Emalı burial had been closely studied from specimens in museums (Starr 1970), the scale of these phases could scarcely be appreciated before their numbers were nearly doubled by the 161 Athenian tetradrachms and 13 decadrachms in the hoard. The number of obverse dies known for tetradrachms alone was increased by more than half, bringing the attested total to 234 and allowing for a statistically estimated original total of roughly 500–600 tetradrachm dies over the approximately twenty-year span from 478 to *c.* 460. If 20,000 coins were struck from each obverse die, the amount of silver minted in tetradrachms alone would have come to 6,600–8,000 talents or 165–200 metric tons. While these estimates are certainly impressive, a better measure of historical significance is the estimated numbers of obverse dies by years. An estimated 500–600 dies in a span of twenty years give an annual average of 25–30 dies per year, which might seem modest until they are compared with the number of dies employed by several of the most productive minting cities among the allied cities of the Athenian *arche*: during the later fifth century BC, the well-studied, annually struck coinages of Abdera, Maroneia, and Samos each employed on average no more than two obverse tetradrachm dies per year. And while these averages remained unchanged, the average obverse die expenditure at Athens continued to increase until in the third quarter of the fifth century Athens was minting silver at a rate approaching a hundred obverse dies per annum (p. 20), meaning that by this time and probably for decades before, far more silver coinage was being minted at Athens than in all of the minting allied cities of the Athenian *arche* put together. Even the wealthiest Greek cities outside of the *arche*, like Syracuse and Corinth, minted their notable fifth-century silver coinages from an average of only two tetradrachm or stater obverse dies annually. Unlike Athens, both of these cities, like most others, were obliged to mint their coins from imported silver.

We will take up these coinages in the following chapters. Our aim here is to emphasize how knowledge of individual coinages is continually being enriched and refined by the discovery of new material, especially in hoards. Where the Emalı hoard fails us (and this is true for the majority of hoards) is in providing any sure clue as to why it was amassed and then hidden. An essentially Lycian hoard, it was probably the treasure of a local ruler. More than half of the silver coins were minted by various dynasts who ruled the small principalities into which the region of Lycia was divided at that time. To this mass of local coinages had been added an abundant mixture of mostly freshly minted silver coinages of the North, East, and Central

Aegean, except for the Thracian tribes, of cities subject to Athens. Perhaps this lot was bagged silver being traded eastward in the Persian empire where the demand for Aegean silver was exceptionally strong. Or it may have originated as a war chest. Although Emalı is not far from the Eurymedon river (see map P.2), the site of a decisive victory by Athens and its allies over the Persians in the early 460s, that was probably not the only Athenian campaigning in the region during that decade. We can be pretty sure, however, that the coins were not booty captured from the Persians; there was no Persian money in it. If the Athenian and allied silver in the hoard were spoils of war, it most likely would have been captured from some unattested Athenian expeditionary force.

In the following chapters we explore how the evidence of coins is able to illuminate and supplement the literary and epigraphical sources for reconstructing the history of the Athenian empire.

2

The Silver Owl Coinage of Athens

They have a fount of silver, a store of treasure in their soil. (Aeschylus, *Persians* 238)

In Aeschylus' play, performed at Athens in the spring festival of Dionysos in 472 BC, eight years after the battle of Salamis, the Chorus of Persians thus responded to the Queen Mother's request for information about the Athenians. The language is poetic, but not exaggerated. The play was a tragedy, yes, but it celebrated Athens' victory over Xerxes, and that victory at sea was won with a fleet made possible because of the rich deposits of silver ore situated in southeast Attica in the mining district of Laureion (Map 2.1).

These deposits yielded silver of an exceptionally high purity, and, far from being merely sufficient for local monetary needs, were so plentiful that from the late sixth century through most of the fourth century BC, Laureion was the largest supplier of silver in the central and eastern Mediterranean world. The silver was disseminated primarily in the form of Athenian owl coins, which became the most highly preferred monetary specie in international trade down to the time of Alexander the Great in the later fourth century. Athens probably exported unstruck silver bullion as well as coined silver, but in either form, or both, its silver was imported in quantity by other Greek states for the minting of their own coinages. Lead-isotope sampling of some of these other coinages has revealed that Laureion silver provided a noticeable portion of the silver in the late sixth- and fifth-century coinages of Aegina, Corinth, Chios, and Samos (Gale, Genter, and Wagner 1980; Hardwick, Stos-Gale, and Cowell 1998). This might seem surprising in the cases of Aegina and, from *c.* 460 BC, Corinth, powers whose relationship to Athens was overtly hostile. But silver, whether in bullion or coined form, was traded as a commodity throughout the Aegean independently of political considerations, and frequently through intermediary carriers.

Early Developments

Athens was one of the first Greek cities to strike and use a silver coinage. But around the middle of the sixth century, when it began to do so, its deep,

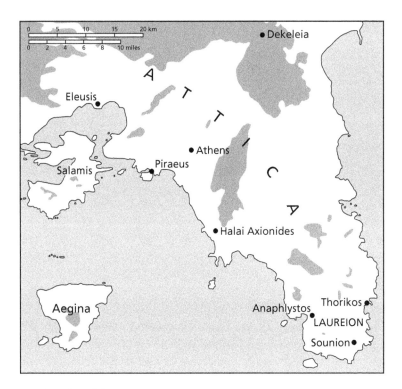

Map 2.1 Map of Attica

rich deposits of native silver were unknown. The city's earliest coins employed a mixture of silver that had come from various sources and presumably had been accumulating in the economy of Athens for some time (Kraay and Emelius 1962, 15–16). Some of this silver was probably local in origin, having been extracted in the Laureion region from shallow seams of low-grade silver-bearing lead ore that had been known and worked from time to time since the Early Bronze Age. These early coins were simple in design, having a pictorial type on one side and a crossed, square punch mark on the other (Fig. 2.1a,b). Changing with each issue of the coinage, the pictorial type identified the issue, but not the issuing city. Since the coins were intended for local use, rarely travelling beyond the borders of Attica, an identifying badge of the city would not have been necessary.

Everything changed in the teens of the sixth century with the discovery, at a far deeper level, of the spectacularly prolific vein of fine ore known to

a.   b.

Figure 2.1 "Heraldic" silver didrachms of **Athens** (*c.* 550–510s BC) with changing obverse types and a punched reverse square with crossed diagonals. (**a**) Obverse of a horse's hindquarters. 8.62 g. *ANS.* (**b**) Chariot wheel obverse. 8.16 g. *ANS.*

Figure 2.2 "Heraldic" silver tetradrachm of **Athens** (510s BC) with a state badge (a gorgoneion, the centerpiece of Athena's aegis [Kroll 1981, 10–11]) on the obverse, and the changing type (here the face and paws of a lion) moved to the reverse. 17.00 g. *Alpha Bank.*

geologists as the "Third Contact." While developing a mining industry to extract and process the metal, the Athenians, in an early instance of their reputation as energetic innovators (Thuc. 1.70.1–1.71.3), radically refashioned the coinage. A new, larger denomination was introduced – the 17.2 g tetradrachm – and after briefly experimenting with coins emblazoned with a state badge in the form of a round gorgon's head (Fig. 2.2), the Athenians transformed the coins by stamping more explicitly national types on each face of the coin: the helmeted head of Athena on the obverse and her accompanying owl and a sprig of her olive tree, together with the three-letter ΑΘΕ abbreviation of the city's name, on the reverse (Fig. 2.3a).

Scholarly opinion is divided on the reason for the change. Some prefer to see it as an expression of the revolution in political organization, namely, the emergence of democracy with the reforms of Kleisthenes *c.* 508 that followed upon the expulsion of the Peisistratid tyrants in 510 (Aperghis 2013, 23; Price and Waggoner 1975, 64–8). Others (notably Kraay 1976, 60) have argued that the decision was economically motivated, to promote immediate recognition of Attic coins in foreign markets in order to strengthen the demand for them. A new sense of Athenian identity obviously accompanied the political revolution, making it tempting to see the

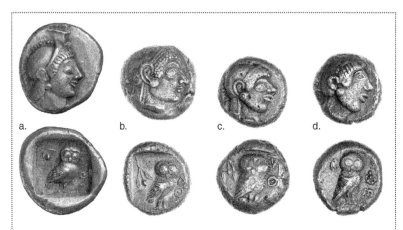

Figure 2.3 Archaic silver owl tetradrachms of **Athens** (*c.* 510s – 480 BC) with the head of Athena wearing a helmet on obverses, and, on reverses, an owl with an olive spray behind its head and the abbreviated ethnic AΘE. (**a**) 17.24 g. *Munich.* (**b**) 16.98 g. *ANS.* (**c**) 16.97 g. *ANS.* (**d**) 17.70 g. *ANS.*

numismatic changes in a political context. But unfortunately we cannot independently pin down the exact date of the design change; it may very well have occurred prior to Kleisthenes' reforms.

Whatever the precise historical context, the changes were influential advances in their own right. Up to this point, Greek coins had been designed in the old-fashioned way with a pictorial type on one face only, and they were either uninscribed or provided at most with a one-letter initial of the minting city. The novel Athena/owl design and three-letter legend however served the practical purpose of ensuring that however far these coins might travel in commerce they would instantly be identifiable as Athenian, making it clear that from the outset the new silver-mining opportunities at Laureion were understood to have important commercial consequences. Athenian silver had quickly become available in surplus quantities, and rather than be traded simply as raw, anonymous bullion, most of it was exported in the form of Athenian money, that is, high-quality silver that carried with it the stamped guarantee of the Athenian state.

As the yield of mined silver continued to increase, the engraving of the coin dies became more hurried, simplified, and repetitious in order to keep up with the available amount of silver to be coined (Fig. 2.3b,c). Moreover, in addition to demonstrating how widely these coins were travelling in international trade, hoards have provided scholars with a large enough sampling of the coinage to give an idea of its staggering scale. According to the most recent estimate, Athenian tetradrachms of the 490s and 480s BC were struck from more than 325 obverse dies. Allowing that an average obverse tetradrachm die had a lifetime production of roughly 20,000 coins (p. 10), this approximation gives a total of over six million tetradrachms, which amounts to more than 4,000 talents (over 100 metric tons) of silver. An indication of the feverish minting at the end of this period is provided by the appearance of the latest archaic tetradrachms (Fig. 2.3d). Their crude die-cutting has been plausibly attributed to "blacksmiths" who were pressed into service when the Athenians had apparently run out of experienced die-cutters in order desperately to mint as much silver as possible for funding the fleet in preparation for the Persian invasion of 480 (Hdt. 7.138).

The Early Classical Coinage (478 to Mid-450s BC)

The Persian invasion devastated Athens: the temples on the Acropolis were destroyed, the city's walls were pulled down; Attica had been overrun. Yet, not long after the defeat and departure of the Persians, Athens resumed coining with the same Athena/owl, types but now, without the emergency caused by an impending invasion, the coins were rendered with much greater refinement and an added detail: the brow of Athena's helmet was now embellished with a row of olive leaves as a kind of victory wreath (Figs. 2.4–2.6). Continuing through several stylistic phases (Starr 1970), these Early Classical owls spanned a little more than two decades and were struck on a massive and ever-expanding scale that by the end surpassed that of the archaic coinage that preceded them. Statistical projections from the current die record of the entire Early Classical coinage in all denominations down to *c.* 455 BC give a minting estimate of more than 9,000 talents of silver, i.e., an amount equivalent to the output of 700 tetradrachm obverse dies.

In the 460s Athens minted didrachms in addition to the usual tetradrachms, drachmas, obols, and hemiobols (Fig. 2.6). And for a few years in that decade, the city experimented with the minting of very large, 43.5 g decadrachms (Fig. 2.5). These imposing coins with a frontal, spread-winged owl on the reverse were minted in some quantity – their production involved at least seventeen obverse dies (Fischer-Bossert 2008). The silver of the one specimen that has been metallurgically analyzed has the diagnostic content (chiefly, a minimal trace of gold) of Laureion silver. If the

Figure 2.4 Early Classical silver owl tetradrachms of **Athens** (478–*c.* 455 BC). Similar types, but with a crown of three olive leaves above the brow of Athena, and, on the reverse, a crescent moon behind the neck of the owl. (**a**) 17.15 g. *ANS.* (**b**) 16.76 g. *ANS.* (**c**) 17.16 g. *ANS.*

Figure 2.5 Early Classical silver decadrachm of **Athens** (early 460s BC). The owl on the reverse stands facing with spread wings; the olive spray and the letters A-Θ-E are positioned at the left and right of the owl's head and legs. 42.13 g. *Alpha Bank.*

Figure 2.6 Other denominations of the Early Classical silver coinage of **Athens** (478–*c.* 455 BC). (**a**) Didrachm. 8.42 g. *ANS.* (**b**) Drachma. 4.27 g. *ANS.* (**c**) Obol. 0.64 g. *ANS.* (**d**) Hemiobol. 0.35 g. *ANS.*

specimen is typical, it means that the decadrachms were not, as once thought, linked to some external windfall, such as precious metal captured from the Persians in the battle by the Eurymedon River in the early part of the decade, but were rather a means for managing the immense output of silver from the mines of Attica (Nicolet-Pierre 1998). By no means unique in the exceptional quality of the design – the tetradrachms produced at this time were equally elegant (Fig. 2.4a) – the sheer size and magnificence of these coins for export could not but have advertised the wealth and power of Athens. Like the similarly large and heavy denominations of silver being minted around this time by Thracian tribes in the north (pp. 77–80), the Athenian decadrachms were convenient for exporting large quantities of the metal (nearly all extant examples come from hoards distant from Athens) or, like the nearly contemporary Demareteion decadrachms of Syracuse, for making payments in large sums (Wartenberg 2015, 360). But with their bulk and high relief they must have been difficult to mint satisfactorily on a mass basis, as is clearly visible from most extant specimens. Inflexible and impractical for any but very sizable transactions, it is not surprising that by the late 460s they were discontinued. Naturally, this contributed greatly to the ongoing rise in the production of tetradrachms.

The "Standardized" Coinage (c. 455–405 BC)

Shortly before the middle of the fifth century the production of the owl silver entered its most voluminous phase by far, as the last of the Early Classical owls gave way to the "Standardized" coinage of the second half of the century (Figs. 2.7–2.9). It has been estimated that nine out of every ten fifth-century owl tetradrachms in museum and private collections belong to this vast mintage. The new coins are characterized by a shift in some details of the reverse: the alpha is elevated so that its upper diagonal touches the side of the owl's head, thetas are normally the same size as the other letters, and the letters altogether are relatively large. No longer tilted, the owls' heads are positioned vertically. On obverses the formerly delicate palmette on the helmet above Athena's ear becomes enlarged and simplified, as if composed of short, linear reeds. And on nearly all of the Standardized coins the front or inner corner of the eye of the goddess is left open, if only very slightly, in a departure from the strictly frontal eyes that are closed at both ends on the Archaic and Early Classical obverses. Some of these modest changes simplified the engraving of the dies; others involved minor artistic

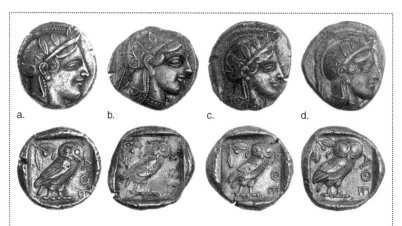

Figure 2.7 Earlier Standardized owl tetradrachms of **Athens** (*c.* 455–440 BC). (**a**) 17.12 g. *ANS*. (**b**) 16.87 g. *ANS*. (**c**) 17.20 g. *ANS*. (**d**) 17.16 g. *ANS*.

updating; but because of the retention of the large, essentially frontal eye of the goddess especially, the coins remained resolutely archaistic in appearance in order to maintain their familiarity and promote acceptance.

The tetradrachms illustrated in Figure 2.7 are typical of the earlier phase of the Standardized minting, a phase characterized by several distinctive forms of the helmet palmette. The phase is well documented in the 142 owl tetradrachms that were buried around 440 BC in the Malayer hoard, a large cache of Greek coins unearthed in western Iran (Appendix B, no. 42). In preparation of a new study of this hoard, Andrew Meadows observes that these owls were minted from 133 obverse dies and represent a relatively small sampling of an original total that by statistical projection possibly involved the use of as much as 100 tetradrachm dies (= *c.* 1,350 talents of coined silver) annually, if the Standardized coinage began in the mid-450s, as is now generally recognized (Kroll 1993, 6). This is an immense leap in production – more than a doubling – from the volume of Early Classical minting mentioned earlier.

What caused this dramatic expansion? Lacking any decisive evidence, we are left to consider three possibilities. One is that the increase may have followed upon the removal to Athens in 454 of the Delian League treasury (p. 4). If the treasury still contained a large reserve accumulated from unspent tribute, including much non-Athenian silver coinage and bullion along with old, archaic Athenian owls, it is plausible that upon moving the reserve, the Athenians might have chosen to remint it into new owls,

Figure 2.8 Later Standardized owl tetradrachms of **Athens** (c. 440–405 BC).
(**a**) 17.16 g. *ANS*. (**b**) 17.15 g. *ANS*. (**c**) 16.09 g. *ANS*. (**d**) 16.97 g. *Oxford*.
(**e**) 17.21 g. *ANS*. (**f**) 17.80 g. *ANS*. (**g**) 17.19 g. *ANS*. (**h**) 16.97 g. *ANS*. The last
coin is a specimen of the so-called Style "M" coins, which some scholars
regarded as Egyptian imitations before a cluster showed up in a hoard in Attica
(Appendix B, no. 5).

which would contain a mixture of Athenian and non-Athenian silver.
While this would have created a dramatic jump in the amount of silver
struck, however, it is unlikely that this single episode could account for the
continuation of Athenian minting at this same unprecedented level over
the next several decades.

A second scenario involving foreign silver is suggested by the cessation
of silver coining by Thracian tribes in the north around the middle of the

a.   b.   c.   d.   e.   f.

Figure 2.9 Silver owl fractions of **Athens,** Standardized type (*c.* 455–405 BC).
(**a**) Drachma. 4.29 g. *ANS.* (**b**) Hemidrachm or triobol. 2.12 g. *ANS.* (**c**) Quarter-drachm or trihemiobol. 1.04 g. *ANS.* (**d**) Obol. 0.69 g. *ANS.* (**e**) Hemiobol, 0.34 g. *ANS.* (**f**) Quarter-obol, 0.17 g. *ANS.* Three of the fractions have denominationally specific reverse types: the owl on triobols (b) stands erect and facing, the owl on trihemiobols (c) stands facing with wings spread, and the quarter-obol (f) is fittingly denoted by a crescent or quarter moon (borrowed from the reverses of Athenian tetradrachms, where the moon accompanies the nocturnal owl).

century, a time that coincides with a strengthening of Athenian influence in the Strymon region in Thrace. If the Athenians were able to gain possession of the silver still being mined in the area, the result, again, would have significantly enlarged the amount of bullion available for minting at Athens but on a sustained basis (pp. 81–2).

The third possibility is that the escalation in coin production was simply the consequence of a greater supply of domestic silver coming from intensified mining in southeast Attica, resulting from improved smelting and new installations for the processing of the ore that allowed previously unworked areas of less rich ore to be exploited (Kakavogiannis 2001; 2005, 331–4). Clearly, this would be the correct explanation if the earlier Standardized tetradrachms should prove to have been struck from Attic silver exclusively. But although there is metallurgical evidence that foreign silver was employed in some of the later Standardized coinage (Flament et al. 2008), no analyses have yet been run on specimens of the earlier Standardized coinage. Much more in the way of elemental and isotopic sourcing of all of the Standardized silver is needed. In the meantime it is worth considering that the increased volume of minting need not be attributable to just one of these hypothetical explanations when it may result from two or all three in combination.

Between hoards of the 440s (Appendix B, nos. 6, 42, 43) and the defeat of Athens in 404, the chronology of the massive Standardized coinage is

Figure 2.10 Part of a hoard of reportedly over a thousand late Standardized Athenian owl tetradrachms, *c.* 400 BC. (Appendix B, no. 50). Found in Asia Minor; now dispersed.

poorly understood. This is owing to the forbidding scale of the coinage itself, the difficulty of identifying coherent stylistic groupings for much of it, and the lack of chronologically anchored hoards. As the volume and speed of production increased, and acceptance of the owls did not depend on stylistic refinements, control of the striking and artistic standards was relaxed. Accordingly, the Athena-head obverses illustrated in Fig. 2.8 and in the large hoard of Fig. 2.10 show relatively little consistency in facial proportions and detail, attesting to the employment of a great number of die-cutters of widely varying abilities and stylistic tendencies (Flament 2007a, pls. 2–23). Apparently, when mediocrity in die-cutting was tolerated and huge amounts of silver had to be pushed through the mint, Athens did not hesitate to employ second- and third-rate craftsmen. This would not be the first time that the appearance of the coinage was sacrificed to the needs of intensified mass production; we have seen it before in the rushed minting before the Persian invasion of 480 (Fig. 2.3d).

Even so, some of the later fifth-century die-engraving is especially odd and produced helmeted Athena heads that are so ill-proportioned and irregular in design that a number of scholars thought that these owls, such as the tetradrachm represented in Fig. 2.8h, were foreign imitations, minted probably in Egypt, where such coins have appeared in quantity and where copies of Athenian owls were in fact struck in the fourth century BC (Buttrey 1982; Robinson 1947, 117; van Alfen 2011, 66–70). Several fourth-century dies for minting imitation Athenian coins have been recovered in Egypt (Meadows 2011b). But nearly all of the uncouth fifth-century coins have proved to be of Attic silver (Flament et al. 2008; Pointing, Gitler, and Tal 2011) and in the 1970s archaeologists excavating at different sites in coastal Attica unearthed two hoards of them mixed with owls of more conventional appearance (Appendix B, nos. 4 and 5). These discoveries demonstrated that such coins, no matter how irregular, routinely circulated in Attica in the late fifth century and should be recognized as genuine products of the Athenian mint (Flament 2011; cf. Arnold Biucchi 2006–2007).

Standardized tetradrachms of these particular styles (known to numismatists as Styles B and M) have also been found in Sicily, including some in a hoard from the destruction of the Sicilian city of Naxos in 403 BC (Appendix B, no. 39). Christophe Flament has suggested (2007a, 80–2, 221–2) that some of these tetradrachms probably arrived in Sicily in the consignments of money sent by Athens to support their expedition against Syracuse. (Thucydides mentions supplementary shipments of 300 talents in the spring of 414 and 150 talents in the summer of 413 [6.94.3 and 7.16.2]). On this hypothesis, the surge in hasty, substandard die-cutting should belong before or around that time, making it tempting to ask whether the surge might have resulted from Athens' program of reminting the silver coinages of its allies into Athenian owls, as authorized by the Athenian Decree on Coins, Weights, and Measures around 414 BC (pp. 111–19). The possibility is worth keeping in mind, even if at present it lacks support from the silver analyses that have been run on owl tetradrachms of the relevant die styles. Once commissioned, the dies in question would have served to strike any silver brought to the mint, including fresh Attic silver bullion as well as foreign and Attic silver that arrived in non-Athenian coins scheduled for reminting. This is another question that calls for a greatly enlarged sample of analyzed specimens.

We learn from the Athenian writer Xenophon (*Revenues* 4.25) that full-scale operations in the Athenian silver industry came to an end in 413 with the Spartans' construction of a permanent fort at Dekeleia in northern Attica (Map 2.1). Historians have usually assumed that among the more than 20,000 Athenian slaves that escaped to Dekeleia (Thuc. 7.27) were many who worked the mines, but one can imagine that another factor was the constant threat of Spartan raids, which would have made continued investment in the mines, slaves, and the open-air processing of ore a very risky business.

Whether the industry at that time was shut down entirely or just seriously crippled – as suggested perhaps by the securing of the mining district with fortifications at Anaphlystos and in 409 at Thorikos (Xen. *Hell.* 1.2.1, with *Revenues* 4.43) – at the mint within the walls of Athens the striking of silver coins continued, making use of whatever silver could be obtained from any source. In 412 the Athenians released the 1,000 talents of coined silver that had been held since the first year of the war as an emergency reserve (but earmarked for a sea attack by the Peloponnesians, Thuc. 2.24.1; 8.15.1). Still, by 407 little silver was left. Between then and Athens' defeat and surrender to Sparta in 404, Athens turned to coining the gold stored as dedications on the Acropolis and to issuing bronze tetradrachms and drachms clad with a thin silver veneer, the debased coinage to which Aristophanes refers in the *Frogs* and to which we shall return in Chapter 7.

Mining, Coining, and Profits

Having surveyed the increases in minting output over the first half of the fifth century, we should now ask, how great was the productivity of the Laureion silver industry at its height? Several rough estimates have been proposed, each from different criteria. From the size of the ancient slag heaps in the Laureion district and the industrial records of the French company that resumed mining in the area in 1903–1908 to extract residual silver and other mineral products, C. E. Conophagos (1980, 138–42, 152, 341–2) estimated that at its fifth-century peak the region was yielding some 20 metric tons (764 talents) of silver annually, a quantity sufficient for the minting of 1.1 million tetradrachms. A higher estimate by at least a third has been posited by Flament (2007c), drawing on Xenophon's statements (*Revenues* 4.23–5) that imply that the slaves who worked the mines and were rented from suppliers at the rate of an obol a day numbered more than 10,000 during the most intensive mining years of the fifth century. Taking the figure of 15,000 slaves, and adding to their hire the estimated cost of feeding and clothing them and of replacing those who died while under contract, Flament calculated that the total annual expense of this workforce alone would have come to about 700 talents. To this the additional costs of processing the ore, refining the metal, procuring charcoal for the furnaces,[1] paying obligations to the state, and the retention of silver for profit could easily bring the total cost that had to be covered by the extracted silver to a thousand talents annually – the equivalent of 1.5 million tetradrachms – a result that Flament regards as a minimum.

Finally, as we have seen (p. 20), an annual output of coins that is still larger by a third has been estimated from the die-to-specimen ratio of the large Malayer hoard lot of Early Standardized owls dating from about *c.* 440 BC, by which time, however, the Athenians may have been incorporating silver from non-Attic sources. Even so, these estimates agree that the magnitude of Athenian coinage surpassed one million tetradrachms annually. Until the vast minting of Alexander the Great in the late fourth century, no other coinage in the ancient world even approached this volume.

Although the Athenian state was solely responsible for the minting of the silver into coins, the extraction of silver from the earth of Attica was a collaborative enterprise that involved massive private participation under governmental oversight and was organized to produce profits in both the public and private spheres. Since the subsurface rights of its territory and hence the silver mines themselves belonged to the state, the state controlled the mining of the silver ore by law, while the actual work of the mining and processing of the silver was performed by private entrepreneurs who, in effect, were licensed by the state. A character's remark of wanting to "buy mines" in Aristophanes' *Knights* (line 362, 424 BC) implies that in the fifth century the mining industry was organized much as it was in the fourth century when many of the administrative procedures are well documented. From fourth-century inscriptions (*R&O* 36) and the Aristotelian *Constitution of Athens* 47.2–4, we know that the state "sold" fixed-term leases of existing mines to private investor-operators for exploitation (Aperghis 1997–98; Kakavogiannis 2005, 334–9). Initially, these leases were modestly priced, but when a mine proved to be seriously productive, its lease was put up for competitive bidding that could bring in relatively large annual

---

[1] T. Rihll (2001, 129, 133) estimates that 16 kg of ore and 18 kg of firewood were required to produce just one drachma (*c.* 4 g) of silver.

returns for the state. When a brand new mine was opened, it had to be registered with the state and any silver produced was subject to a tax of one-twenty-fourth (4.16 percent), a low rate that was probably maintained to encourage investing in the risky business of exploring for new ore deposits.

One commentator has argued that Athens' income from fees and taxes at the various stages of silver extraction and processing may not have been as generous as the size of the industry might lead one to expect (Davis 2014, 266–4). However, the truth of the matter is that we just do not know how much of the newly recovered silver was taken by the state. Michele Faraguna suspects that the mine operators may have been contractually obligated to turn over to the state more than 10 percent of their acquired silver in addition to any leasing fees they had paid (Thür-Faraguna 2019, 49–54). But however large the state's share of the silver, all of it would have been brought to the mint to be converted into coined money. And so, presumably, would be the share kept by the private operators as well, so that they could meet their high operating expenses and take their profits in cash. At the mint the city collected additional revenue through an exchange or minting fee of (very probably) 5 percent that covered the cost of minting and provided additional profit to the government (pp. 115–16).

Once coined, much of the miners' coined silver initially had to be spent in Attica, compensating the host of middlemen, money-lenders, and tradesmen on whose goods and services the industry depended. However, the most expensive necessities – slaves, which were rented out on contract from local suppliers (Xen. *Revenues* 4.14–15), the grain to feed them, and firewood for the great amount of heat needed for the processing of ore – had to have been procured and imported from distant ports, meaning that a large part of this minted silver was passed on directly or indirectly for such purchases abroad.

Commerce and Imports: Consumer Culture

Although it is impossible to know how much was removed from Attica in this and other long-distance trading, Athens' owl silver was the city's most valuable item of export. Aristophanes' *Frogs* of 405 boasts it was "valued by Greeks and barbarians everywhere" (pp. 131–2). A critical source is Xenophon's *Revenues*, which, though written in the mid-fourth century, states a fact applicable to the fifth century in its emphasis that Athenian silver coins were always worth more abroad than at their source.

Xenophon on the Exportability of Attic Silver

In most port cities merchants have to take on a return cargo because the local coinage is of no use elsewhere. At Athens, however, not only are there more desirable things to export than anywhere else, but even if merchants do not want to load up with a return cargo of goods, by exporting the coinage they will be exporting an excellent item of trade; for wherever they sell it, they will everywhere get more than they invested.

Revenues 3.2

Apart from *Frogs*, however, extant fifth-century textual sources are silent about exports from Athens. Rather, they fixate on Athens' importing power (Kallet 2007, 81–5) – though if we only had more than several isolated fragments of Aristophanes' comedy, *Merchant Ships* of the second half of the 420s, we might be able to revise that statement. A famous fragment from a lost play of similar date by Hermippos, another comic poet (fr. 63, *apud* Athen. 1.27e–28a) lists a staggering series of luxury, strategic, and basic commodities imported by the shipowner Dionysos.

The Imports of the Shipowner, Dionysos

Muses who live on Olympos, tell me now about the good things
that Dionysos brought here to men on his black ship
Ever since he first set out over the wine-dark sea.
From Cyrene he brought stalks of silphium and oxhides;
From the Hellespont, mackerel and all kinds of salt fish;
From Thessaly fine cereal and beef ribs; . . .
The Syracusans offered pigs and cheese. . . . From Egypt came
hanging sails and papyrus for writing; from Syria, frankincense.
Beautiful Crete sends us cypress wood for the gods' temples,
Libya, offers an abundance of ivory for export,
and Rhodes sends raisins and figs that bring sweet dreams.
Next, from Euboea, come pears and delicious apples,
From Phrygia we get captive slaves, from Arcadia, mercenary soldiers.
Pagasae in Thessaly provides us with servants and branded slaves.
Paphlagonia sends us chestnuts and
fresh almonds, the prized delicacies of a feast.

From Phoenicia come dates and fine flour,
and from Carthage, rugs and elegant pillows.

Trans. J. Henderson, in Rusten 2011, 170–1, adapted

In the Funeral Oration composed by Thucydides, Perikles boasts that *"the size of our city attracts every sort of import from all over the world, so that our enjoyment of goods from abroad is as familiar as that produced here"* (2.38 trans. Hammond, adapted). Finally, in an anonymous treatise by a writer dubbed the "Old Oligarch" because of his cranky, anti-democratic slant, comes this fuller variant of Perikles' statement: *"It is because of their command of the sea that the Athenians have mingled with peoples in different regions and discovered a wealth of delicacies. Whatever is tasty in Sicily, Italy, Cyprus, Egypt, Lydia, Pontus, the Peloponnese, or anywhere else – all these have been brought back to Athens because of its command of the sea"* ([Xen.] 2.7). These sources convey well the vibrant "consumer culture" of imperial Athens (van Alfen 2016).

Democracy and Empire

We have more evidence about the use of money by private individuals at Athens than we do for any other city in the Greek world. Such use is implicit in the aforementioned passages, but in addition there is a wealth of documentation about internal taxation as well as revenue from the empire, and the symbiotic connection in the Athenian mentality between Athens' democracy and empire: money is siphoned off from the empire and used to support the democracy.

This evidence comes principally from Old Comedy. Its richness comes from its topicality and its obsession with money – where it comes from, where it goes, who gets it, whether the ordinary citizen or those in power, the demagogues like Kleon. In a precious section of Aristophanes' *Wasps*, produced in 422, a son is moved to convince his father, a juror who is addicted to his daily pay of three obols, that they are peanuts compared to the amount of money that the city has. (Comic exaggeration is at play with respect to the total income claimed by the son.)

Loathekleon: Then listen, pop, and relax your frown a bit. First of all, calculate roughly, not with counters but on your fingers, how much tribute we receive altogether from the allied cities. Then make a

> *separate count of the taxes and the many one-percents, court dues,*
> *mines, markets, harbors, rents, proceeds from confiscations. Our total*
> *income from all this is nearly 2000 talents. Now set aside the annual*
> *payment to the jurors, all six thousand of them . . .We get, I reckon,*
> *a sum of 150 talents.* (Lines 655–663, trans. Henderson, Loeb Classical Library)

The obsession with money in private and public life in fifth-century Athens was something Plato, writing in the fourth century, found noxious: "Perikles made the Athenians "money-grubbers" – literally "silver-loving" (this was not a compliment!) – (*Gorgias* 515E), because he introduced jury pay in order to allow ordinary Athenians to participate in the running of the government. The Aristotelian *Athenaion Politeia* (24) goes into more budgetary detail:

> *They provided abundant maintenance for the many, so that more than*
> *twenty thousand men were supported from the tribute, the taxes and*
> *the allies. There were 6,000 jurymen, 1,600 archers, and, also 1,200*
> *cavalry; 500 members of the Boule; 500 guards of the dockyards, and*
> *also 50 guards on the Acropolis; up to 700 officials at home and about*
> *700 overseas. In addition to these, when the Athenians later went to*
> *war they had 2,500 hoplites; 20 guard ships; other ships sent out for the*
> *tribute . . . employing 2,000 men selected by lot; also those at the*
> *Prytaneion, orphans; and the jail guards. All these were paid from*
> *public funds.*

Now, the author states that the funds all came from taxes and the tribute. And there may be exaggeration, or a mistake over the number of offices abroad (the 700 is thought to be a doublet from the number of offices internally). But the point here is that a hallmark of Athens' democracy was payment for offices held in order that those below the elite could afford to participate – and there was a presumption that the empire furnished the funds and made possible the democratic way of life.

The mint supplied the drachmas and smaller fractional coins needed for most of these payments in huge numbers (Fig. 2.9). To the regular provision of drachmas (4.3 g), triobols (= hemidrachms), obols (0.72 g), and hemiobols, in the second half of the fifth century the Athenians added the quarter–drachma (= 1½ obols) and eventually diobols. Subsistence living required one or two obols a day. The citizens who served by the hundreds on the large Athenian juries received two obols a day until the pay was raised to three obols by Kleon in the 420s. Hoplite infantrymen, rowers, and laborers (slave or free) normally, until later in the Peloponnesian war (when after the Sicilian disaster and during the fortification at Dekeleia, the rowers' rate was halved), received a daily wage of a drachma a day.

Dispersal within the *Arche*: Tribute, Payments, and War

Besides this domestic use and its role in export in and beyond the Aegean, we can assume that a demand for Athenian coinage existed also among the cities of the Athenian *arche*, if only as the preferred specie for the payment of tribute to Athens. Whether some of the cities might have paid in non-Athenian silver coinages, or even in silver bullion, is uncertain, but it is surely possible, especially in the early years of the alliance when the institution of tribute was still in its infancy and Athenian coinage may not have been abundant enough for cities to acquire it in the necessary quantities to meet their obligations. If the cities were able to pay these obligations in whatever silver currency they chose, the *Hellenotamiai* who received the funds, rather than having to calculate the equivalence in Attic silver of a multiplicity of coinages of diverse weight standards, varying exchange values, and complications arising from inconsistent wear and potential weight loss, very likely treated all non-Athenian silver money alike as plain bullion by weight (see Appendix A.2). In Athens silver bullion was worth less than coined Athenian silver, probably by the difference of 5 percent. Still, the most satisfactory arrangement from an Athenian point of view would have been to welcome payment in Athenian currency as much as possible, not only because of efficiency in collection and recording but also because it brought in money that could be expended immediately, without exchange, in military operations and other Athenian expenses. For those cities that had no coinage of their own, it would have made sense to pay in Athenian coins. Many cities that did mint may have found it to their economic advantage to do likewise when they were able to obtain Athenian coinage through transactions and favorable exchange rates.

The largest public expenditures of Attic coinage were made by the Athenian state for military purposes, such as the purchase of timber and other materials for building and equipping warships (Psoma 2015), the continual payments to the rowers in the fleet – the manning of a single trireme cost a talent per month (200 men earning a drachma a day) – and the remuneration of soldiers who served in campaigns like the two-year siege of Poteidaia (432–430), on which the Athenians spent some 2,000 talents (p. 83). This evidently was not an abnormal sum for such extended military operations, like the sieges of Thasos in the 460s and of Aegina in the 450s, both of which lasted also for two years; the much shorter nine-month siege of Samos (440–439) cost over 1,400 talents (O&R 138; *AIO*; see also Thuc. 1.116–17). Since the troops and rowers purchased their food and supplies abroad wherever they happened to be, and because many of these men were from allied states (Trundle 2016, 77–9) and brought their earnings home after campaigning, there is ample reason to assume that much of this Athenian money entered local economies throughout the *arche* through exchange with local currencies or acceptance alongside them. And then there were the Athenian officials who were sent out to the cities and received their payment from Athens, and the thousands of Athenian cleruchs settled on expropriated lands throughout the empire. Presumably they would have preferred to take and use as much money from home as they could.

Testimony to the owls' Aegean-wide influence is to be found in references to money that the Persian satraps Tissaphernes and Pharnabazos, as well as Cyrus, employed in paying the rowers of the Spartan fleet in the last years of the Peloponnesian War. In several passages where Thucydides (8.29.1, 8.45.2) and Xenophon (*Hell.* 1.5.1–7) give exact figures for the rowers' daily salaries, the sums are expressed in Attic drachmas and obols, implying that Athenian currency had become the common money for accounting and pay in Aegean naval affairs (see Chapter 7). The mercenary rowers in the Peloponnesian fleet were drawn from all over Greece, and they were used to being paid in Athenian money. Although their wages could be paid in other currencies – as they were when the funds furnished by the satraps ran out and the Spartan admirals were forced to pay with local coinages obtained from Chios and other Greek cities (p. 128) – an episode related in Plutarch's *Life of Lysander* indicates that in the last year of the conflict the war chest of the Spartan commander Lysander was supplied with large quantities of Athenian owls. The episode concerns the bags of these coins that were left unused when the war was over and reminds us that, with respect to money, its value is almost always more important than its origin, even when minted by an enemy.

Bags of Athenian Owls from Cyrus and Lysander (404 BC)

What remained of the moneys, together with all the gifts and crowns which he had himself received . . . Lysander sent off to Lacedaemon with Gylippus, who had held command in Sicily. But Gylippus, as it is said, ripped open the sacks at the bottom, and after taking a large amount of silver from each, sewed them up again, not knowing that there was a writing in each indicating the sum it held. And when he came to Sparta, he hid what he had stolen under the tiles of his house, but delivered the sacks to the ephors, and showed the seals upon them. When, however, the ephors opened the sacks and counted the money, its amount did not agree with the written lists, and the thing perplexed them, until a servant of Gylippus made the truth known to them by his riddle of many owls sleeping under the tiling. For most of the coinage of the time, as it seems, bore the effigy of an owl, owing to the supremacy of Athens. (Plutarch, *Life of Lysander* 16.1–2 (trans. Perrin, Loeb Classical Library)*

In the following passage, Xenophon (*Hell.* 2.3.8) provides a more detailed account of the spoils of war that Lysander delivered to the Spartans but makes no mention of Gylippos, which is understandable if the latter's treasure ship was sent ahead separately (as also in the version of Diodoros 13.106.8–9).

Lysander then sailed back to Sparta with the Spartan ships, taking with him the prows of the ships he captured, the triremes from the Piraeus (except for the twelve that the Athenians were allowed to keep), the crowns that he had received from the cities as gifts for himself, 470 talents of silver, which was the amount left over from the tribute money which Cyrus had assigned to him for prosecuting the war, and whatever else he had acquired during the war. All these things he gave to the Lacedaemonians just as the summer was ending. At this point the war was over. (Trans. Marincola, adapted)

When taken together, the two passages imply not only that the funds that Lysander had received from Cyrus in 405 were largely, if not entirely, in the form of Athenian owls, but also that, since this money was raised in tribute from cities under Cyrus' control (as stated in Xen. *Hell.* 2.1.14), the cities had been paying their quotas of Persian tribute in bags of Athenian silver as well (Thompson 1964, 122).

Figure 2.11 Athenian-type silver tetradrachms minted by Persian authorities (late fifth or early fourth centuries BC). (**a**) On the reverse, at the right of the owl's feet, a miniature head of the Persian King, bearded and wearing a crown, 16.45 g, *Karlsruhe*. (**b**) With the head of a Persian satrap (or the King?) on the obverse, and, on the reverse, an owl, and the letters ΒΑΣ, an abbreviation of *basileus*, the Greek word for "king". 15.31 g. *London*. From a hoard in South Central Asia Minor (Appendix B, no. 51).

a.

b.

That Persian rulers had become used to employing Athenian coinage by the end of the fifth century and continuing into the fourth, mainly in their dealings with Greek mercenary forces, is readily seen from a number of imitation owl tetradrachms that Persian authorities minted themselves, such as the two illustrated in Fig. 2.11. The first (a) is discretely "signed" with the tiny crowned head of the Persian king at the feet of the reverse owl. But there is nothing discrete about the second (b): a hybrid coin with the head of the Persian king or satrap (Tissaphernes?) replacing the head of Athena, and the three-letter abbreviation ΒΑΣ (for the Greek word, *basileus* = king), explicitly informing that the coin was issued in the name of the Great King (Alram 2012, 72–73).

The foregoing considerations lead one to envisage Athenian coinage as an increasingly influential coinage that, owing to its voluminous scale of production, its commercial familiarity, and central role in military and imperial finance, circulated in the Aegean in quantity, even as large amounts were simultaneously being drawn off to remote destinations. Accordingly, it ought to have had a significant impact on the minting of local coinages by the cities allied with Athens, and for this, as we shall see in the next chapter, there is good evidence.

Hoards and Dispersal beyond the *Arche*

There is, however, a complicating factor, namely, the minimal supporting evidence of hoards within the *arche*. Excluding the hoards of Attica and the neighboring island of Euboea, which was closely tied to Athens by proximity and settlements of Athenian cleruchs, out of the remaining twenty-eight hoards known from the *arche* (see Appendix B, nos. 9–36), only two contained Athenian silver, nos. 28 (Olynthos, with a single Athenian drachma) and 33 (Ionia, with a single Athenian fraction). Can it be, as Koray Konuk (2011) has cautioned, that the dissemination and importance of Athenian silver in the *arche* was in fact relatively limited?

The answer depends on whether the existing hoard record must be regarded as decisive evidence for circulation, and here the four relevant hoards recorded from Attica (Appendix B, nos. 2–5) raise considerable doubt, for this is a paltry total for a region that for the whole of the fifth century was flooded with its own coinage. By and large, scholars have sought to ascribe the dearth of reported hoards to a former lack of interest in recording and preserving large finds of owls because of the tediously repetitive character of the coinage; such coins were more profitably melted down. On the other hand, Jonathan Kagan (2008, 109) following Russell Meiggs (1972, 169), observes that "[t]he stability of the Athenian hegemony in this period was not conducive to abandoned coin hoards."

However that may be, the contrast with the known hoards of Athenian tetradrachms outside of the empire could hardly be more glaring (Appendix B, nos. 37–55; Map 2.2). Hoards of Athenian tetradrachms from Eastern Asia Minor, the Levant, and Egypt are the source of most of these tetradrachms in museums and private collections today. The numbers are staggering: more than 6,000 owl tetradrachms from an early fourth-century hoard found at Tel el Maskhouta, Egypt; a reported total of 10,000 owls from a hoard understood to have been recovered in 2007 in North Syria; a hoard of over 1,300 Standardized owls from a hoard probably from Turkey; and the list goes on. As this book was being readied for publication, reports began to circulate about the largest find of Athenian tetradrachms yet known: some 16,000 owls (the equivalent of ten talents) in a hoard of 24,000 silver coins that was recently discovered in coastal Southeast Asia Minor and was already being dispersed in trade (Appendix B, no. 45).

As these finds make clear, the strongest and most lasting demand for Athenian coinage lay in the non-Greek world beyond the Athenian Aegean.

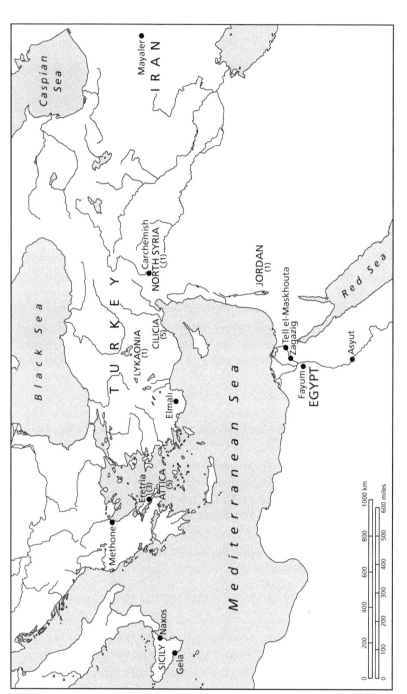

Map 2.2 Hoards with a significant component of Athenian coins

Although the insatiable appetite for Greek silver had been drawing great quantities of Greek coins and silver bullion into Egypt and the East since the sixth century, in the second quarter of the fifth century imports of mixed Greek silver coins gave way to an increasing preference for silver coins stamped with Athena/owl types, which came to be more highly valued than other silver (Fig. 1.3). In some parts of Egypt and the Levant they came to be recognized as the sole or preferred form of money, as we know from written Egyptian accounts beginning in 412 BC that record sums in "Greek staters" (Agut-Labordère 2016, 5; Kroll 2001, 14–15) and from the Athena/owl imitations that were minted in Egypt and Palestine in the fourth century (Meadows 2011; Tal 2012; van Alfen 2011; see Fig. 2.12). Many of the exported owls were shipped from Athens directly to markets outside of the Aegean, for instance, to Egypt for the purchase of grain, papyrus, and linen for the sails of ships. From the very beginning of the owl coinage, Athens was always able to mint in surplus quantities for export. In addition, during the course of the fifth century much of its coinage that was dispersed in the Aegean through trade and, especially, its hugely expensive military and naval operations, would have migrated to the East through commercial channels. We have no way of knowing how much Athenian money was lost in unsuccessful expeditions into Persian territory, like the disastrous intervention in Egypt in the 450s (Thuc. 1.104, 109); some of these failures would have resulted in the loss of whole war chests.

One noteworthy feature of the massive Eastern hoards of fifth-century owls is that a majority (Appendix B, nos. 47–55) were assembled and buried at the very end of the fifth century and in the first decade or two of the fourth, which is to say after the power of Athens had collapsed. This implies that earlier there had been a real need for Athenian coins among Athens' subject allies, in large part a public need that would have restrained private hoarding in the Aegean and the foreign market demand that sought to draw owls away. As Matthew Trundle (2016, 75) has

Figure 2.12 Palestinian imitation of a silver Athenian tetradrachm (late fifth or early fourth century BC). The West Semitic letter *shin* on the cheek of Athena is the mark of a mint in Philistia. 16.52 g. *ANS*.

explained, silver owls within the *arche* flowed out to its periphery and commonly returned to the center in a cyclical process and were "more likely to have not found themselves in hoards because of their constant use within the system." With the defeat of Athens in 405/404, however, the need for owls as the essential money of the empire suddenly came to a halt. Except, of course, at Athens itself, all owls on hand that were not melted down for new coinages in a new Greece under Spartan domination were freed up for trading that brought them to the remote lands where the demand for them was unlimited.

Thus, in the fifth century, Athenian coinage became a dominant currency in two great and fundamentally independent spheres outside of Attica itself. The larger sphere was the silver-hungry world beyond the Aegean – of Egypt and the Near East – where Athenian owls began to appear already in the Archaic period and where they continued to be drawn after the *arche* collapsed. Notably, this distant demand for Athenian silver had hardly anything to do with Athens' political power. For most of the fourth century, abundant hoards and local imitations of Athenian owls attest that in these lands employment of this coinage had become even more popular than before. This phenomenon attests not only to the coins' abundance and reputation for quality but also to the self-generating dynamic that causes particular currencies, once they are commonly accepted, to create for themselves ever-expanding levels of preference in trade and savings. As there was little in the way of local currency in Egypt and much of the Near East at this time, and always a want of good silver, Athenian silver served to fill these voids.

This was unlike the case in Athens' *arche*, the other sphere of Athenian monetary dominance. Expended in payments from Athens and returned in payments to Athens in tribute, rents, and other obligations, the silver coinage of Athens became the coinage of its empire. But it was far from being exclusively so. Most of the major cities of the *arche* had been minting and using coinages of their own since the later sixth or early fifth centuries, and minting continued at some of the cities for the duration of the *arche*. Let us now turn to these coinages in the next chapter, ultimately to see what impact Athens and the increasing volume of circulating Athenian coinage exerted on them.

3

Coinages of the Allied Cities

To Mint or Not to Mint

When we leave Athens and turn to the coinages minted by the member cities of the *arche*, we enter the vast, diverse, and highly particularized world of the Greek city-states, each with its separate traditions, its own economic and political interests, and, for those that had the means and incentives to mint a coinage, their own money. Of the approximately two hundred communities known to have been subject to or allied with Athens (in contrast to the many more that were sometimes claimed by Athens), only sixty-eight are known to have minted coins between 478 and 404 BC, that is, roughly one-third. The majority of these were wealthier cities, that is, those that were assessed more than one talent in annual tribute payments to Athens (see Table 3.1). But even among the minting cities, relatively few coined continuously, or even with occasional intervals, from the 470s into the last decade of the century. Many minted only in minor, fractional denominations for one or more brief periods. All of these coinages nevertheless were minted for the practical purpose of serving as currency in the public and private sectors of a city's economy (plus in a few exceptional cases for export), while enabling the minting city normally to profit from its legal control of this currency, as we shall see. Since initiating a coinage was costly – a city had to procure the necessary stocks of metal and the services of skilled die-cutters and workmen, including slaves – it is understandable that some smaller centers might prefer to use the coins of neighboring cities, especially if the cities were part of a regional commercial network, or in the case of highly traditional agricultural communities to rely on older exchange practices employing agricultural goods. Minting, once undertaken, might be discontinued if it proved economically disadvantageous. And it is important to remember that the closing of a mint did not mean an end to the circulation of the coinage that it had struck; unless called in, the coins, though in an increasingly worn state, might remain in use for decades.

In this chapter we survey a large sampling of the allies' coinages with two goals in mind: first, to give some idea of the coinages' tremendous range of diversity and interest, and, second, to determine what impact Athenian coinage and political power may have had on local civic minting over time. As can be seen at a glance from this chapter's illustrations, these civic coinages differed greatly in appearance. Since acceptance of a coin usually depended upon its familiarity, there was a strong practical incentive for many minting cities to resist changes in their coins' designs. To take two extreme examples, the silver coins of Chios and Aegina retained their rudimentary, archaic format down to the end of the fifth century BC: both coinages remained uninscribed and continued to be stamped on one face only with a simple pictorial device to identify the issuing authority – a sphinx for Chios (Fig. 3.22) and a turtle for Aegina (Fig. 4.3). Beginning later, the owl coinage of Athens introduced a more developed format, with pictorial types stamped on both sides and the addition of the city's name inscribed in abbreviated form. Once introduced, the format is found elsewhere, as in the later, more refined staters of Ainos on the north Aegean coast (Fig. 3.17a), which also represented on obverses the head of the city's protecting deity and on reverses an attribute of the deity in a display of civic piety that became increasingly typical of Greek coinages in later centuries.

Apart from employing such divine imagery, cities sometimes chose to identify themselves on coins with references to the agricultural products for which they were best known. This is especially true for major producers of wine, as we see on coins of Naxos, Terone, Mende, Aphytis, Maroneia, and Chios, with their varied depictions of grape clusters and vines (Figs. 3.10, 3.12, and 3.16b), wine vessels (Figs. 3.6a, 3.8, 3.10c, and 3.22), and, at Mende, even a drinking Dionysos (Fig. 3.10b). These and other images stamped on civic coins were chosen as expressions of a city's self-image, but their primary role was economic: the stamps certified the legitimacy and value of the issuing state's coins.

Fifth-century innovations in the designing of coins included an expansion in the amount of lettering inscribed on the coins and attention to administrative accountability. By the middle of the century it was becoming common to inscribe the name of the issuing city in full, usually by referring to it collectively as the people of the community. Typically, we read on a coin of the city of Abdera on the northern rim of the Aegean that it is a coin "of the Abderites," i.e., "of the people of Abdera" (Fig. 3.15a). In some of the more elaborate, continuously minted coinages, each issue came to be distinguished by means of an adjunct symbol and, as in the case of Abdera and the neighboring city of Maroneia, the inscribed name of the responsible minting official was added as well (Figs. 3.15 and 3.16b). These names and issue symbols served as "signatures" of the officials who supervised the striking of the issue or batch of coins and who were therefore legally accountable for the accuracy of the coins' weights and quality of metal. Apart from this administrative purpose, the recording of their names on the coins was a way of honoring these citizens for performing this service for the city.

Λ further area of variation – and one that can appear especially forbidding to anyone encountering it for the first time – is to be found in the coinages' weight standards and denominational structures. As listed in Appendix A, at least ten different weight systems are represented in the allies' coinages. Originating before the era of coinage when precious metal was weighed out in the form of bullion, some of these systems became regional, like the Aeginetan system with a stater (the large, base denomination) of 12.4 g that came to be employed for nearly all coinages of the Peloponnesos, central Greece, and the Cycladic islands; or the Euboean system (stater of 17.2 g), the dominant weight system of the cities of Euboea and of the Chalkidic peninsula in northern Greece that had been settled from Euboea. From its home in western Asia Minor, the Milesian standard (stater of 14.2 g) owed its scattered dissemination around the Aegean to the enterprise of early Milesian traders. The smaller denomination coins of most of these standards were divisions of sixths (*hektai*), twelfths (*hemihektai*), and tiny twenty-fourths (*half-hemihektai*) of the stater. The alternative denominational terms "drachma" and "obol" (= one-sixth of a drachma) emerged from a separate metrological tradition and rose to prominence through their use with Aeginetan and Athenian coinages. Although the Attic weight standard (drachma of 4.3 g) and denominational structure ultimately became the most widely employed in the Greek world from the time of Alexander the Great, it was only rarely adopted by cities within the Athenian empire (e.g., Samothrace, Fig. 3.17b; Ialysos, Rhodes, Fig. 3.27b) until the 430s, and then chiefly in a cluster of fractional coinages minted by smaller cities in north-west Asia Minor (pp. 96–8). Occasionally a city might change its coin standards to accommodate changes in political alignment and/or the trading networks to which it belonged (see pp. 99–102).

Finally, the civic coinages of the *arche* differ with respect to their metal – either silver or electrum (an alloy of gold and silver) – and the coinages' intended range of circulation and use. To a considerable degree, metal and circulation were linked since nearly all Greek coins of the fifth century were struck from silver and, as we noted earlier, were ordinarily minted for local, internal use. This applied to large-denomination coins as well as to small ones, which might weigh as little as one- or two-tenths of a gram and were far more commonplace in the silver currencies of these cities than the illustrations in this book have been able to indicate. Exceptionally, for much of the fifth century the city of Mytilene on the island of Lesbos minted its local, lower-value coinage in an alloy of silver and copper known as billon (Fig. 5.3a). And late in the century, bronze itself began to be adopted very gradually as a monetary metal for representing minimal values like quarters and eighths of a silver obol (Fig. 4.13).

Coinages in Electrum

At the far other end of the monetary spectrum were the coinages of electrum that a few cities in the northeastern region of the Aegean minted in surplus quantities mainly for export since these coinages satisfied a demand for high-value coins that enjoyed international recognition. They were also favored for hoarding and savings, as we learn from the following account of the famed Athenian speechwriter and orator Lysias (12.10–11).

> I went into my bedroom and opened the strong box ... On seeing its contents, Peison told two of his servants to take what was in it ...three talents of silver coin, four hundred kyzicenes, a hundred darics, and four silver drinking cups.

A victim of the "Thirty Tyrants," Athenian oligarchs installed in Athens by the Spartans in 404/3, right after the city's capitulation to the Spartans at the end of the Peloponnesian War, Lysias had offered to pay money (a ransom, in effect) – a talent, a handsome sum – in return for his life. But once his savings were discovered, the entirety was confiscated.

This passage gives us a glimpse of the kind of wealth that a very well-to-do resident of Athens kept in a metal-clad chest in the innermost room of his house. Lysias' three talents of silver would have been in the form of Athenian tetradrachms, some 4,500 of them – an astonishing private reserve. In addition to these and some fine silver vessels, his accumulation included 500 gold and electrum gold coins, whose value if measured in silver would have come to the impressive sum of two and a third talents.

The gold coins have a special interest because of their high value and recognized international acceptability. Although darics were pure gold coins of the Persian king (Fig. 7.2a), they circulated quite commonly in Aegean Greece during the late fifth century, especially after 412 when Persian gold began to finance the Spartan war effort. In addition to showing up in private hands, many darics are listed in inscribed Athenian treasury accounts of the last third of the century (*TN* 145, 147, 150 = *IG* I^3 383, 386–9, largely restored). A hoard of reportedly several hundred was found in Athens (*IGCH* 322; second quarter of the fourth century [Nicolet-Pierre 1996]).

The other "gold" coins in Lysias' savings were the electrum staters from Kyzikos (Fig. 3.1), the major port city on the Propontis (or Sea of Marmara) and a member of the Athenian *arche*. Kyzikos profited by minting these coins for use in the maritime trade of the region and the Black Sea, where the coins became the exclusive currency for purchasing wheat in the grain markets of the Crimea and the northwestern Black Sea coast. Although staters of Kyzikos were referred to as gold coins, they were not, like darics, minted from pure gold (in the fifth century Greek cities did not mint in pure gold except in rare emergencies; see Fig. 7.8), but, as mentioned earlier, from a gold-silver alloy. Weighing 16.1 g, a Kyzikene stater had a value of six or seven Athenian tetradrachms (as did, approximately, the all-gold Persian daric that weighed 8.5 g).

During the *arche*, great quantities of Kyzikene staters were paid in tribute, as evidenced by the entries of the one-sixtieth paid to Athena. In the first inscribed tribute quota list (*TN* 135 = *IG* I^3 259, 454 BC), payments in silver and in Kyzikene electrum gold were totaled separately. This speaks to Athenian accounting practice, but it makes clear that kyzikenes were recognized as legitimate tender for use alongside silver. Indeed, in inscribed fifth-century Athenian financial accounts generally, kyzikenes are by far the most abundant of all non-Athenian currencies listed (*TN* 138–54). An entry of state expenditure in 418/17 (*TN* 138 = O&R 170) includes a disbursement of at least 4,000 staters of Kyzikos to the commanders (*trierarchs*) of warships operating off the coast of Argos. Since much of this pay for the fleet personnel was to be exchanged wherever the squadron put in for provisions, it is evident that by that time international recognition of this currency extended even to the Peloponnese. The other electrum staters listed in Athenian financial records were those minted by the city of Lampsakos on the Hellespont (Fig. 3.2). Seventy-four of them were included in the funds for the building of the Parthenon in the 440s (*TN* 154 = *IG* I^3 436). In 409/8 the Treasury of Athena in the Parthenon held 1,408 of them, presumably as a reserve currency (*TN* 140 = *IG* I^3 376, lines 95–96).

A final important electrum-gold currency was the coinage of one-sixth staters or *hektai* minted jointly by two other members of the *arche*: the cities of Phokaia on the Ionian coast and of Mytilene on the island of Lesbos, each city striking in alternate years (Figs. 3.3 and 3.4). Part of the minting agreement between the two cities survives in an inscription and

a.   b.   c.   d.   e.

Figure 3.1 Electrum staters of **Kyzikos** (fifth century BC). The obverse types changed with each (usually annual) issue, but all are "signed" at the bottom with the city badge, a small tunafish. Phokian standard. (**a**) Obverse type of a sow. 16.13 g. *ANS*. (**b**) Helmeted head of Athena. 16.06 g. *Oxford*. (**c**) The Athenian Tyrannicides, Harmodios and Aristogeiton, holding swords and preparing to strike. 15.91 g. *ANS*. (**d**) The founder and first king of Athens, Kekrops, depicted with the lower body of a snake, holding the original olive branch of Athena. 15.96 g. *Paris*. (**e**) The goddess Earth (Ge) lifting up the earth-born baby and future king of Athens, Erechthonios. 16.05 g. *London*. The last four Kyzikene obverse types are among several that were chosen because of their explicit Athenian imagery; the last three depicted famous statues in Athens (Abramzon and Frolova 2007, 21). See pp. 140–1.

Figure 3.2 Electrum stater of **Lampsakos** (*c*. 500–450 BC). "Troad" standard. Unlike the other electrum coinages with types that change with each issue, the staters of Lampsakos have a stable civic type: the forepart of a winged horse within an encircling vine wreath. Above the horse on this particular specimen is the administrative mark of a pellet. 15.12 g. *ANS*.

a.   b.

Figure 3.3 Electrum *hektai* of **Phokaia** (fifth century BC). Phokian standard. These Phokian sixths are stamped with a figural type on their obverses only. On (**a**) is depicted the head of a ram and, below, a seal (*phokē* in Greek), the civic badge of Phokaia. 2.61 g. *ANS*. (**b**) displays a head of Athena wearing a helmet ornamented with a griffin. 2.55 g. *ANS*.

a.   b.   c.

Figure 3.4 Electrum *hektai* of **Mytilene** (*c.* 500–427 BC), with a type on each side. Phokian standard. (**a**) The types are the helmeted head of Athena and, on the reverse, two confronted calves' heads. 2.51 g. *ANS*. (**b**) shows the forepart of a bull and, in sunken relief, the head of a lion. 2.52 g. *ANS*. On (**c**) is a young male head with horns (Pan or Aktaion?) and the face of a gorgon. 2.51 g. *ANS*.

specifies that any minting official who knowingly adulterated the electrum alloy was to be punished with death (*TN* 348, O&R 195, Mackil and van Alfen 2006, 210–19). Generally equivalent in value to a silver Attic tetradrachm, these *hektai* circulated regionally, chiefly in NW Asia Minor, along the shores of Hellespont, and the Propontis.

Besides being made of electrum, the metal alloy employed in the late seventh and sixth centuries for the earliest coinages of Western Asia Minor, the aforementioned coins continued three other traits of these early coinages: all are uninscribed, most have a typeless punch reverse, and, with the exception of the staters of Lampsakos, the types with which the coins were stamped changed from one issue to the next, each type corresponding to the term of office of the minting official who was personally responsible for maintaining the correct proportion of the issue's silver-gold alloy. The type thus served as a kind of signature of the minting official, who normally had the privilege of choosing the type himself (Kroll 1981, 3–8).

Far more significant, however, was the circumstance that these electrum coinages served as *common* (in Greek, *koina*) currencies, coinages that enjoyed, if not universal acceptance everywhere, then at least ready acceptance within very large commercial zones. We find the term only in Plato, who in a discussion of money for his ideal state (*Laws* 5.742a–b) distinguished between two types of coinage: a local (*epichorikon*) coinage that was to be used in everyday transactions and was acceptable as legal tender only within the state which produced it, and a common (*koinon*) Hellenic coinage for military expenditures (such as mercenaries) and for use by citizens when they needed to travel or to do business abroad. Actually, both kinds of coinage are found decades earlier at Kyzikos, Lampsakos, and Mytilene: although these high-value electrum coins could be employed at home as well as away, for everyday domestic use, each of the cities also minted lower value coins of silver (or in the case of Mytilene, of a silver-bronze alloy). The silver coins of Kyzikos were very small fractions; some of Lampsakos were as large as a drachma (Fig. 3.18a).

Silver Coinages

We have noted that most Classical Greek poleis produced their silver currency for their own use, like most nation-states today. And, like present-day states and monetary unions, most maintained a closed currency system. When a traveller crossed into the territory of a polis, he was obliged to exchange the coins he brought with him for local coins, the only coins accepted by merchants and city officials. This was a matter of law. As we learn from surviving inscriptions from Athens, Olbia, Gortyn, and Smyrna (Kroll 2011a, 231n9), cities that used their own coins passed legislation to ensure that these coins would be officially recognized as the sole legal tender in the state and that they had to be accepted. Such legislation tended to make the coinage more valuable in the state that issued it than elsewhere, as did the modest overvaluation of the coins that states added as a minting charge. All of this explains Xenophon's observation (p. 25) that the coinage of most cities was strictly local and was not useable elsewhere, nor profitable to export (and why Athenian coinage was exceptional in this regard). It also helps to explain why many cities chose to mint their own coinage, as it was understood to be a potential source of state revenue. Since port cities obtained their largest share of revenue from harbor and custom taxes, it was to their advantage to collect these taxes in their own currency and to require visitors to exchange their foreign coin for the local silver. Not only did this greatly simplify the collection of tax money but also the need for exchange effectively meant that foreigners were obliged to buy the over-valued local coinage at a premium that the cities could legislatively control, if they wished. Any foreign silver that was taken in exchange could be passed on to the state for reminting into its own money or sold to dealers who specialized in precious metals or foreign currencies.

Overvaluation and the legally protected exclusiveness of local coinages also served to keep local silver coins from being drawn away from the city. As is borne out by finds in excavations and hoards, silver coins of a drachma or less in value are rarely distant from their city of issue. Large-denomination silver coins, however, did travel from time to time, as shown by those that were buried in distant hoards, or were overstruck at some distant mint, or were recorded in financial inventories at Athens. But that does not mean that these coins could be used routinely as currency at these destinations, only that they had been carried there for any number of reasons, for example, by travelers who knew that they ultimately would have to exchange the coins wherever they went, or by merchants who, rather than pay exchange fees to money changers, privately negotiated deals with the foreign coins they had on hand, or who might simply trade these coins as bullion, that is, as a precious-metal commodity.

Against this background of the conventional, domestic purpose of civic coins, certain silver coinages nevertheless came to be accepted more widely in regional trade or monetary zones. In the fifth century the silver staters of Thasos and Ainos were deployed as trade coinages with the markets of inland Thrace and became so popular there that they were imitated and adopted by the inhabitants (pp. 56, 59). This kind of regional acceptance on a vastly larger scale in the Greek world explains the early external expansion of Aeginetan and the electrum coinages.

Collectively, the coinages of the member cities provide a kind of pictorial atlas of the far-flung Athenian empire and for that reason alone are worth reviewing. As historical documentation, however, nothing about them is more informative than their patterns of minting in a political and monetary environment dominated by Athens. Of the nearly seventy allied silver coinages within the *arche*, we can give only an illustrated sampling, with emphasis on the major coinages and those that have been most reliably studied. Table 3.1 gives a full list but no details other than characterizing a city's coinage by the size of its highest denomination and by one of three broad temporal categories. These are as follows:

(*A/a*) Coinages of cities that minted continuously or intermittently over the duration of the *arche* or as long as the minting city remained a member of the *arche*. Nearly all these coinages began before the formation of the *arche*, in the late sixth or early fifth century, and most were struck in large, stater-size denominations along with one or more smaller denominations (*A*). Some, however, consisted only of drachma-sized coins and/or fractions (*a*).

(*B/b*) Coinages of cities that had also begun to coin before 478 but continued to do so only for a limited span, generally down into the 460s or the 450s BC. These coinages, too, were mostly struck in both large and small denominations (*B*), but some consisted of drachmas or below alone (*b*). After a gap of inactivity some of

these suspended coinages were resumed in small denominations, occasionally (as at Methymna on Lesbos) with new types
and weight standards, much later in the century.

(C/c) Coinages of states that did not strike during the *arche* until
around or after the middle of the fifth century. Almost invari-
ably, these coinages were smaller denomination coinages
(c) and date in the great majority of cases to the time of the
Peloponnesian War. Although most of these late-minting cities
had never coined before, a few had originally produced a short-
lived coinage in the late sixth or very early fifth century prior to
the formation of the *arche*.

Coinages of all three temporal types are found in most regions of the
arche, with the exception or partial exception of three notable concen-
trations. First, the coinages of the cities in greatest proximity to Athens,
namely, those of Euboea and the Cycladic islands, were uniformly Category
B/b coinages whose minting did not last much, if at all, beyond the 460s.
Second, a majority of the long-term Category A minters is to be found far
from Athens in the north, along the Aegean coasts of the Chalkidike and
Thrace. Finally, a unique concentration of small-denomination coinages
was minted by allied cities in the Troad and Aeolis in the northeast corner
of the *arche*, especially in the later fifth century (Category c).

In the following survey the allied coinages are grouped according to the
geographical regions or districts that the Athenians used administratively
themselves, in particular for the recording of the cities' payments of tribute
(Table 3.1).

The Island District

Euboea

An early end to minting is hardly surprising for Chalkis, Eretria, and
Karystos, the three coining poleis of Euboea, the wealthy, elongated island
that almost touches the northeastern coast of Attica (Fig. 3.5). Metrologically their coinages were related to the coinage of Athens through the
common use of the 17.2 g Euboeic weight unit. Before *c.* 480 Eretrian coins
especially are found with Athenian ones in hoards in both Attica and
Euboea. After 447 BC, when the cities of Euboea revolted – unsuccessfully –
from Athens, the city tightened its control over the island and distributed
large tracts of land to Athenian settlers (cleruchs). Three hoards of

a.   b.

c.

Figure 3.5 Silver coins of Euboean cities (*c.* 500–465 BC). Euboean-Attic standard.
(a) Stater of **Chalkis**, depicting an eagle carrying a snake; on the reverse is a wheel,
with the abbreviated name of the city, X-A-Λ, in letters of the Chalkidian alphabet.
16.68 g. *Lanz 111 (2002), 116.* (b) Didrachm of **Karystos**, depicting a cow and,
on the reverse, a rooster and the initial letters of the city name, KA. 8.21 g. *ANS.*
(c) Didrachm of **Eretria**, depicting a cow, with initial E; on the reverse, an octopus.
8.48 g. *ANS.* The bovine obverse types refer to Euboea, the name of which means
"rich in cattle." The other animal types are badges of the cities.

fifth-century Athenian coins, predominately tetradrachms, have been
unearthed in Euboea (Appendix B, nos. 6–8), with the earliest implying
that by the middle of the century Athenian currency had mostly replaced
the local coinage and was responsible for the cessation of local minting.

The Cycladic Islands

With the exceptions of Delos, whose Attic-weight coinage was discontinued
soon after 478, and Kythnos (Fig. 3.7c), the Cycladic cities of the *arche* that
minted (Sheedy 2006) did so on the Aeginetan standard, the common trade
standard in the southern Aegean in the later sixth century when these
coinages began. Conflicts with Athens were probably involved in bringing
the prolific minting of the wealthiest of these islands, Naxos and Paros
(Fig. 3.6), to an end (Kagan 2008). After it attempted to secede around 470,
Naxos was crushed by Athens and, as Thucydides puts it, "enslaved" (by
which he meant that the Naxians lost their autonomy and means of defense

a.   b.

Figure 3.6 Silver coins of Cycladic cities. Aeginetan standard. (**a**) Stater of **Naxos** (to *c.* 470 BC), depicting a wine cup (kantharos) with grape clusters hanging from each handle and an ivy leaf above, all symbols of Dionysos. 12.3 g. *ANS*. (**b**) Drachma (= half stater) of **Paros** (to *c.* 465 BC) with the state badge of a goat. 6.06 g. *ANS*.

a.   b.

c.

Figure 3.7 Silver coins of Cycladic cities. Aeginetan and Attic standards. (**a**) Aeginetan-weight stater of **Siphnos** (460s BC), with head of Apollo and, on the reverse, an eagle in incuse square, in the corners of which a leaf or grain of wheat and letters of the abbreviated ethnic, Σ-I-Φ. 11.86 g. *Paris*. (**b**) Siphnian coin of the same design and date but at *c.* 4 g the equivalent of both an Aeginetan one-third stater and an Attic drachma. 3.84 g. *ANS*. (**c**) Attic-weight drachma of **Kythnos** (*c.* 475–460 BC), with a boar's head obverse. 3.66 g. *ANS*. Kythnos had minted coins of this type and *c.* 4 g weight since the late sixth century, without other coins of conventional Aeginetan weight to go with them.

and became tributary subjects of Athens; Thuc. 1.98.4); two decades later Athens imposed a cleruchy of 500 Athenians on the island. Paros never revolted, but in the 460s Thasos, its powerful island colony in the north Aegean, did so and failed after a lengthy siege. Thasos had gold and silver mines of its own, as well as control over other mines and coastal *emporia* on the Thracian mainland. Whether or not Paros' extensive series of drachms (Fig. 3.6b) had been minted at Thasos or from silver supplied from it, the colony and mother city were so closely tied that Athens' reduction of Thasos and takeover of its mainland possessions could only have had serious repercussions for the Parians. This is speculation, but it is tempting to see the crushing of Naxos and Thasos (and the appropriation of further sites belonging to Paros or Thasos along the Thracian coast) as having a bearing on the punishing amount of tribute Paros paid – one of the highest assessments in the *arche*, from sixteen, and beginning in the late 440s, eighteen talents in the accounts of a few years. Alternatively the tribute imposed may have been determined chiefly by the island's profits in exporting the finest marble in the Greek world.

In contrast to the turbulent early relations of these cities with Athens, the other island cities of the *arche* that minted had no such troubles, yet they, too, closed their mints either before 470 (Delos and the three cities on the island of Keos) or probably in the 450s (the island polities of Kythnos and Siphnos). The coinage of Siphnos is especially informative, since in the early 460s, after having minted an Aeginetan-weight coinage for several decades, the Siphnians introduced a newly designed coinage of Aeginetan-weight staters (Fig. 3.7a) with a reverse format adopted from Athenian decadrachms (Fig. 2.5): a spread-winged bird – here an eagle – with the three letters of the abbreviated ethnic in three corners of the enclosing incuse square and a vegetal leaf or kernel in the fourth corner, at the left of the bird's head.

These *c*. 12 g staters were accompanied by a second denomination of *c*. 4 g (Fig. 3.7b). Coins of this last weight had already been struck on Kythnos (Fig. 3.7c). Although the unit was equivalent to four Aeginetan obols or a third of an Aeginetan stater, it is not found anywhere else as an Aeginetic denomination. The weight was first and foremost Athenian – the weight of the Attic drachma – and its adoption at Siphnos, along with appropriately adjusted fractions (Sheedy 2006, 49–50), all evidently to be used with coinages of both standards in a mixed currency system, implies that Athenian tetradrachms had not only begun to circulate there in quantity but that the Siphnian state formally recognized their integration. Since this influx of Athenian money would only have increased over time, it would have made no economic sense for the city to go to the trouble of continuing to mint a competing coinage of its own. This example can be taken to apply to other minting cities as well, even when evidence for the local integration of Athenian coinage is lacking. After minting the larger Apollo-head denominations of the 460s, the Siphnians coined smaller ones exclusively (obols and 0.6–0.5 g hemiobols) for a few years before closing their mint altogether, in a pattern that was repeated in other allied cities.

The total cessation of local minting in the islands, including Euboea, by mid-century, however, is unmatched in any other region of the *arche* and, as mentioned earlier, provides a good illustration of the effect of proximity to the central power of Athens. That membership in the Athenian alliance and the end of minting were connected is underscored by the example of Melos, the one Cycladic island polis that steadfastly refused to submit to Athens. Melos continued to mint staters of its own (Fig. 6.1) until 416, when Athens captured it and replaced its population with Athenian colonists.

The Thraceward District

The Chalkidike Peninsula

We move now from the center of the Aegean to its northern and eastern rim, beginning in the northwest corner with the large three-fingered peninsula known as the Chalkidike. Rich in metals, timber, and excellent soil for viticulture, the peninsula was populated by no fewer than fifty-three member cities of the Athenian *arche*, the great majority of them founded by colonists from Chalkis and other Euboean poleis. The region's numismatic history during the Peloponnesian War complements and enriches the literary testimony of Thucydides on its changing politics, first, engineered by Perdikkas II, king of Macedon, and then enlarged by the Spartan general Brasidas.

In the late sixth and early fifth centuries, nine of these cities minted coinages of staters, *hektai* (sixths), and smaller fractions of Euboean weight. By 480, the number of minting cities had dwindled to five, of which three fall under Category *B*: Terone and Skione, which coined in staters with fractions into the 460s (Hardwick 1998, 125) and 450s, respectively (Fig. 3.8a,b), and Poteidaia, whose coinage after 480 or so was restricted to *hektai* alone (Fig. 3.8c).

The two major minters in the Chalkidike were the cities of Akanthos and Mende, both of which coined all the while that they were subject to Athens (Category *A*). With access to the silver mines in the northeastern part of the peninsula, Akanthos produced the more prolific coinage (Fig. 3.9). Apart from the addition of the inscribed ethnic on reverses, the design of its staters remained unchanged over the course of the century even after 424, when Brasidas persuaded the Akanthians to revolt from Athens. While

a.

b.   c.

Figure 3.8 Silver coins of cities in the Chalkidike, Thrace (*c.* 480–450 BC). Euboean standard. (**a**) Stater of **Terone**, showing a wine amphora ornamented with bunches of grapes 16.81 g. *ANS*. (**b**) Stater of **Skione**, showing the head of the city's founder Protesilaos, wearing a helmet that is inscribed with his name along the crest; in the reverse square is the stern of his ship and, at the corners, the letters of the abbreviated ethnic Σ Κ Ι Ο. 16.75 g. *Alpha Bank*. (**c**) *Hekte* of **Poteidaia**, depicting Poseidon Hippios, holding a trident, on horseback; beneath the horse is the letter *pi*. The head of a woman (an Amazon?) wearing a conical headdress on the reverse. 2.76 g. *ANS*.

retaining their design, however, Akanthos switched from minting on their traditional Euboeic standard (*c.* 17 g) to the lighter (*c.* 14 g) Milesian standard (Fig. 5.9). The Akanthians remained independent of Athens for the rest of the war. Along with the Chalkidians at Olynthos, the city continued to supply Milesian-weight coins, largely, it is assumed, in support of forces opposing Athens.

The coinage of Mende is renowned for its exquisite Dionysos staters and fractions that relate to the city's fame as a producer of an exceptionally fine and widely exported wine (Fig. 3.10a,b). The coinage ran down to the Spartans' brief takeover of the city in 423. After being retaken by Athens the next year, the city continued minting down to 405, but it did so, in keeping with a shift observed elsewhere in the *arche*, in no denomination larger than a *hekte* (Fig. 3.10c) (Kagan 2014, 17–9).

In the second half of the fifth century, three communities of the Chalkidike allied with Athens minted coins for the first time under the

Figure 3.9 Silver coins of **Akanthos** to 424 BC. Euboean standard. Of the two staters,
(**a**) [16.95 g. *ANS*] dates before, and (**b**) [16.79 g. *ANS*] dates after *c.* 460 BC, when the
ethnic AKA-N-ΘIO-N ("of the Akanthians") was added around the reverse square.
The obverse type of a lion mauling a bull is a distinctively Near Eastern design. It
implies that the coinage commenced soon after 515 BC, when the Chalkidike was
subjugated by the Persians. (**c**) *Hekte*, showing the forepart of a bull with turned
head. 2.66 g. *ANS.* When in 424 the Spartan general Brasidas persuaded the
Akanthians to revolt from Athens, they continued to mint with the same types and
denominations but on the lighter Milesian standard (Fig. 5.9).

arche (all Category *c*). One of these coinages was the horse/eagle
hektai signed by the "Chalkidians" (Fig. 3.11a); since these coins are of
traditional Euboean weight, they should date before 432, when the associated populations of small Chalkidian towns moved to Olynthos, revolted
from Athens, and issued *hektai* on the lighter Milesian standard of
their patron, King Perdikkas II. (We will return to these changes in the
coinage of cities in this region in Chapter 5.) The other new minting cities
were Aineia (Euboean *hektai*, Fig. 3.11b), which had not coined since
the 490s or 480s, and Aphytis, one of Athens' staunchest allies in the
region and the base for Athenian naval and military operations during
the siege of Poteidaia (p. 83). At *c.* 2.0 g the coins of Aphytis (Fig. 3.12)
are so light when compared with the *hektai* of these other mints that they
have been plausibly identified as Attic-weight hemidrachms (Kagan
2014, 19n).

Figure 3.10 Silver coins of **Mende**. Euboean standard. Of the two staters, (**a**) dates before and (**b**) dates after the redesigning of the coinage around 460 BC. The obverse of (**a**) shows an ass carrying a bunch of grapes and the abbreviated ethnic MENΔAI inscribed above from right to left. 17.31 g. *ANS*. On the obverse of (**b**) Dionysus reclines on the ass and holds out a wine cup; a bird sits on a branch in front; the vine laden with grapes on the reverse is framed by large letters of the full ethnic MEN-ΔA-I-ON ("Of the Mendaians"). 16.77 g. *ANS*. (**c**) is a *hekte* and dates after 423 BC, when Mende had stopped minting staters; the wine amphora on its reverse is accompanied by the inscription MEN-ΔA-IH (= "Mendaian [sixth]"; Kagan 2014, 15–8). 2.63 g. *ANS*.

Figure 3.11 Silver coins of allied cities in the Chalkidike dating after *c.* 450 BC. Euboean standard. (**a**) *Hekte* of the **Chalkidians** (at **Olynthos**) before revolting from Athens in 432, showing on the obverse a galloping horse, and on the reverse the blazon of Chalkis in Euboea (cf. Fig. 3.5a), an eagle holding a snake in its beak. The letters in the corners of the incuse square (barely legible on the present specimen) read counterclockwise from the upper left corner X-A-Λ-K in the old, local alphabet of Euboean Chalkis, which many communities of the Thracian Chalkidike regarded as their founding city. 2.63 g. *ANS*. (**b**) *Hekte* of **Aineia**: head of Aeneas, wearing helmet; on the reverse the ethnic (clockwise, beginning at the upper right corner) A-I-N-E-AΣ around a four-part square. 2.32 g. *ANS*.

enlarged

Figure 3.12 Coin of **Aphytis**, showing the Head of Ares, and on the reverse a vine of grapes in a frame (as on the reverses of nearby Mende) with the ethnic AΦY-T-AIO-N ("Of the Aphytaians"). Weighing 1.96 g, it is likely to have been struck as an Attic hemidrachm around the time that Athens was using the city as its naval base for the siege of Poteidaia, 432–430 BC. *ANS.*

Coastal Thrace

Strung along the northern rim of the Aegean between the Chalkidike and the Hellespont were seven prominent cities of the *arche* that owed much of their wealth to their strategic position as commercial intermediaries between Aegean Greece and a major source of precious metals, timber, and slaves, the Thracian hinterland. Three of the cities were Category *B* or Category *b* minters: Neapolis (Fig. 3.14), Dikaia (Fig. 3.16a), and Samothrace (Fig. 3.17b). The rest (all Category *A*) coined in large and small denominations until very late in the *arche* and call for special attention.

The staters of the island polity of Thasos (Fig. 3.13) are unusually interesting, and not only because of their lively type that relates to the imagined wild, Dionysiac revels in the Thracian mountains. After Thasos was defeated by Athens at the end of its revolt, the Thasians appear to have increased their commercial connections with the interior of Thrace. We know this from material, not literary evidence. Hoards and Thracian imitations of these coins have been found in quantity in Bulgaria (Picard 2011, 83, 86–88; Psoma 2011, 145), demonstrating the strong demand for this coinage in inland Thrace and helping to explain why the type and the uninscribed, single-face format of the coins, having become familiar externally, were kept unchanged through three stylistic (and two metrological) phases to the end of the fifth century.

In contrast to this Thasian conservatism, the staters minted by the polis of Abdera (Fig. 3.15) were among the most advanced coinages of fifth-century Greece insofar as each emission was identified by the name of an annual administrative official and by an issue symbol that changed with

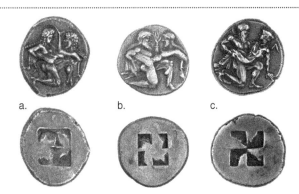

Figure 3.13 Silver staters of **Thasos** with the scene of a satyr carrying off a nymph. (a) Stater of full Parian-Thasian weight (late sixth century to Thasos' failed revolt against Athens in 465–463 BC). 9.21 g. *ANS*. (b) Stater with a more naturalistic version of the type – the open hand of the struggling nymph is shown with all five fingers – struck around the middle part of the fifth century at a reduced 8.6 g weight (the equivalent of an Athenian didrachm or Euboeic half-stater). 8.38 g. *ANS*. (c) Stater of the refined, classical third phase with a relaxed nymph, her hand behind the head of the now solicitous satyr, dating from sometime in the last quarter of the fifth century. 8.73 g. *ANS*. As known from Thasian inscriptions on stone, these coins continued to be called staters and were minted with sixths and twelfths as earlier.

Figure 3.14 Silver stater of **Neapolis** (*c.* 480–460 BC). Parian-Thasian standard. Designed with the face of a gorgon, a popular image on earlier Greek coins because of its convenient, circular shape; in origin it was a device for scaring away dangerous spirits. 9.69 g. *ANS*. The port city of Neapolis (modern Kavalla) is situated on the Thracian mainland opposite Thasos, its founder.

each change of name. Since the recording of annual names and symbols began close to 450 and involved some 40 issues, the coinage is seen to have run with little or no interruption down into the last decade of the fifth century (Kagan 2014, 20). In the later fifth century, the neighboring city of Maroneia also added the name of an annual magistrate to each issue of its coinage (Fig. 3.16b). The parallelism with Abdera extended to the 14.7 g weight standard of the two coinages and allows that Maroneia was probably striking into the last years of the *arche* as well (Kagan 2014, 20; Psoma 2008, 158–67).

a.   b.

Figure 3.15 Silver staters of **Abdera**, with the obverse city badge of a griffin facing left. "Reduced Chian" standard (Psoma 2015, 181). On (**a**), an issue of the third quarter of the fifth century, the magistrate's name, ΚΑΛΛΙΔΑΜΑΣ (Kalllidamas), and issue symbol, a tunafish, are shown around and below the griffin; the ethnic on the reverse reads ΑΒΔΗΡΙΤΕΩΝ ("of the Abderites"). 14.84 g. *ANS*. On (**b**), an issue of the last quarter of the century, the official's name, ΗΓΗΣΑΓΟΡΑΣ (Hegesagoras), and the issue symbol, a youthful male head, have been moved to the reverse. 12.85 g (sic). *ANS*. A griffin facing right was the state badge of Teos (Fig. 3.23c), the Ionian city that founded Abdera.

a.   b.

Figure 3.16 Other silver coins of coastal Thrace; "reduced Chian" standard. (**a**) Half-stater of **Dikaia** (*c.* 480–465 BC), with the city badge, a head of Herakles, and, on the reverse, a rooster. 7.21 g. *ANS*. (**b**) Stater of **Maroneia** (last quarter of fifth century BC). On the obverse is the state badge of a running horse, with the issue symbol of a star and, below, the abbreviated ethnic, ΜΑΡΩΝ; the reverse inscription in the frame around vine with grapes reads ΕΠΙ ΜΗΤΡΟΔΟΤΟ, "during (the magistracy of) Metrodotos." 13.84 g. *ANS*.

The chronology of the coinage of Ainos, the last major minting city along the Thracian littoral, was entirely different. Not beginning until *c.* 460, its first phase of staters (Fig. 3.17a) ran to the middle of the century and was accompanied by a long series of fractions, mostly *hektai*, followed by a small phase of staters in the last third of the century, but exactly when is unclear (Figueira 1998, 130–4). Crude imitations (May 1950, 279–80) attest to the popularity of these staters among the inland Thracian tribes far

a.   b.

Figure 3.17 Silver coinages of Eastern Aegean Thrace. (a) Stater of **Ainos** (*c.* 460–450 BC). The head of the city-god Hermes on the obverse is accompanied on the reverse by Hermes' goat, a Silenus mask administrative symbol, and the abbreviation AINI (for "of the Ainians"). 16.81 g. *ANS*. May (1950, 265–9) and others (Davis and Sheedy 2019, 17–20) identify the stater as a triple siglos, but its subdivisions imply rather that the staters were of reduced Euboean-Attic weight (p. 149). (**b**) Hemidrachm of **Samothrace** (second quarter fifth century BC), with the types of a seated sphinx and the head of a lion. Attic standard, 2.11 g. *ANS*.

up the Hebros river from Ainos. Whereas the 16.5 g weight standard of the Ainos staters is still under discussion, the far more modest coinage struck by the island polis of Samothrace (didrachms through half-obols) is notable for being a coinage of exact Attic weight (Fig. 3.17b).

While we may conveniently group these coinages of littoral Thrace together geographically, one cannot help but be struck by their decidedly visual and metrological diversity, a reminder of their local origins and functions. Such diversity characterizes also the coinages of the regions that follow.

The Hellespontine District

Gold mines in the northwestern corner of Asia Minor, one of which is still being worked today, were responsible for the most significant monetary production in this region, namely, the striking of coins in electrum, discussed earlier. The four great electrum mints – Kyzikos on the Propontis, Lampsakos on the Hellespont, Mytilene on the island of Lesbos, and Phokaia on the Ionian coast – extend in a curve from north to south. Most civic minting in the region nevertheless was in silver, and ordinarily in denominations of modest size, like the Category *b* drachmas of Lampsakos and Abydos on the Hellespont (Fig. 3.18a,b) and the still smaller silver denominations of Parion (Fig. 3.19a), Selymbria (Fig. 3.19b), and Kyzikos,

a.   b.

Figure 3.18 Silver coinages of two Hellespontine cities, Persian standard (470s–440s BC). (**a**) Drachma of **Lampsakos**, with a janiform (i.e., double-faced) female head on the obverse and the head of Athena and a caduceus (an administrative symbol) on the reverse. 4.67 g. *ANS*. (**b**) Drachma of **Abydos**, with the city emblem, an eagle, and the ethnic (running counterclockwise around the eagle) ABY[ΔH]NΩN ("of the Abydeans"); on the reverse, the face of a gorgon. 4.81 g. *ANS*.

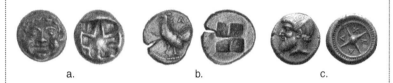

a.   b.   c.

Figure 3.19 Silver coinages of three Propontine cities. (**a**) Drachma of **Parion** (first half fifth century BC), with a gorgon-face obverse and a rough cruciform pattern in the square on the reverse. Uncertain standard, 3.93 g. *ANS*. (**b**) Drachma of **Selymbria** (first third fifth century BC) depicting a rooster on the obverse with the abbreviated ethnic in the local dialect ΣΑ. Persian standard. 4.36 g. *ANS*. (**c**) Drachma of **Kalchedon** (second half fifth century BC), showing a bearded male head (the seer Kalchas?) and on the reverse, a wheel with the letters K A Λ X between spokes. Attic standard, 3.80 g. *Oxford*.

all on the Propontis. A majority of these silver coinages came to be minted on the Persian weight standard, a phenomenon that should be attributed to patterns of commerce in the area. The Attic standard shows up again at Kalchedon (Fig. 3.19c) across from Byzantion at the mouth of the Bosphoros.

Immediately to the south in the Troad several allied cities – Assos, Kebren, Skepsis (Fig. 3.20a–c), Lamponeia, and Gargara – began to coin in very small denominations, mostly obols, before the middle of the century. Although the weight standard of most of these coins has yet to be identified, when after the failed revolt of Mytilene on Lesbos in 428–427 the coinages were rejuvenated under the influence of new Attic-weight coinages in the area, these cities switched to Attic, creating in this northeast corner of the *arche* a genuinely Attic currency zone (pp. 96–8).

a.   b.   c.

Figure 3.20 Three small-denomination silver coinages of the Troad (second quarter of the fifth century BC). (a) Drachma of **Assos**, depicting a seated griffin and on the reverse a lion's head. "Troad" standard, 3.35 g. *Oxford.* (b) Hemidrachm of **Kebren**, with the types of a ram's head and the face of a gorgon. 1.75 g. *CNG (2014).* (c) Hemidrachm of **Skepsis** with the ethnic ΣK-A-ΨI-ON ("of the Skapsians") around a winged horse, and on the reverse a pine tree and the retrograde letters N-E. 2.07 g. *Oxford.* The weight standards of the last two coinages require further study.

a.   b.

Figure 3.21 Silver coinages of island cities off the Troad. (a) Stater of **Tenedos** (first half fifth century BC), with the obverse type of a janiform head: bearded male face on the left, a woman's face with earring at the right; reverse with a double-blade axe (the state badge of Tenedos), the abbreviated ethnic [T]-E/N-E, and the symbol of a cup. "Troad" standard, 7.59 g. *Oxford.* (b) Stater of **Methymna**, Lesbos (*c.* 480–460 BC), depicting a charging boar and on the reverse the head of Athena with a Pegasos ornament attached to the brow of her helmet. The ethnic is inscribed on both sides, preserved only in part at the top of the obverse; on the reverse it reads MAΘYMN-AIOΣ ("Mathymnian") in front and behind the head. Euboean standard, 8.34 g. *ANS.*

Remaining fiercely independent of its rival, Mytilene, the city of Methymna on the northern coast of Lesbos minted in two series, one with the standard and subdivisions of the Euboean weight system in the first half of the fifth century (Fig. 3.21b) and then, after a considerable gap, a second series with entirely different types (Athena head in a Corinthian helmet/ Lyre), curiously, on the lighter Samian standard (p. 149). Adding to this mix of coin standards in the northeast corner of the Aegean and beyond, Tenedos, advantageously located as the first island on the busy shipping lanes from the Hellespont to all points in the southern Aegean, minted its fifth-century coinage (Fig. 3.21a) on what is believed to be a "Troad" standard (p. 149).

The Ionian and Karian Districts

Among the several Category A silver coinages minted by cities on the coasts and islands of Ionia and Karia, historically the most important were the nearly continuous coinages of Chios and Samos, both wealthy islands that provided manned warships to the Athenian fleet instead of tribute, although Samos lost its favored status after a failed rebellion in 440–439 when it was, first, compelled to pay a war indemnity and, subsequently, tribute.

Chios minted a two-denomination coinage on its own standard: staters and (after *c.* 435) thirds (Fig. 3.22). Minting also on a weight standard of its own, Samos struck two long series of 13.1 g tetradrachms with occasional smaller denominations (Barron 1966, 48). The first, consisting of tetradrachms mostly marked with symbols denoting the separate issues, ran from the 470s down to the 440 rebellion. A few years after Athens suppressed the revolt, minting resumed with the second series of twenty-two tetradrachm issues consecutively numbered in letters of the alphabet

a.   b.

Figure 3.22 Silver (**a**) stater and (**b**) one-third stater of **Chios** (third quarter fifth century BC). Chian standard. The obverse type of both – a seated sphinx facing a wine amphora, with a bunch of grapes above – is the badge of the island state. 7.78 g. *ANS.* 2.39 g. *ANS.*

Figure 3.23 Silver tetradrachm of **Samos** (*c.* 430 BC). Samian standard. The obverse depicts a lion's scalp, the reverse the forepart of an ox in front of an olive branch. The abbreviated ethnic ΣΑ is inscribed above the ox; the numeric letter gamma below the ox's neck identifies the issue as no. 3 in an annual series. 12.85 g. *ANS.* The lion scalp and ox are associated with the Samian worship of Hera; the olive branch alludes to the island's signature product: fine olive oil.

a.   b.

Figure 3.24 Silver coins of Ionia BC, Milesian standard. (a) Drachma of **Ephesos**, with a bee (an attribute of the city goddess, Ephesian Artemis) and letters E – Φ on the obverse (second quarter of fifth century). 3.24 g. *ANS*. (b) Obol of **Miletos** (later fifth century BC), depicting a lion head and on the reverse a floral-star design representing the sun. The lion and the sun were both associated with the city god, Apollo. 1.09 g. *ANS*.

(Fig. 3.23). These ran from *c.* 434 to 412 BC, when, following the disaster that Athens suffered in Sicily, Samos became the home base of the Athenian fleet in the eastern Aegean. Accordingly, the Samians raised the weight of their tetradrachms to the Attic standard (p. 131; Fig. 7.9). This is a valuable instance of a coinage exemplifying an historical circumstance known from the written record. Chios, on the other hand, had become the first of Athens' allies to rebel and join up with Sparta after the Sicilian expedition. Chios provided payments in its own money to crews of the Spartan fleet on at least three occasions and, in connection with such financial arrangements, as we shall see (p. 128), altered the denominational structure of its silver coinage (Fig. 7.3) and even minted in electrum (Fig. 7.4).

Ephesos probably remained an active minter during the *arche* until its defection in 412; it struck drachmas at least into the 460s (Fig. 3.24a), as well as infrequent staters, and a great number of fractions, some minuscule (*c.* 0.15 g) (Konuk 2002, pl. 6). On the other hand, Miletos, which had issued a massive quantity of twelfths or obols (*c.* 1.2 g) in the late sixth and early fifth centuries revived this coinage (Fig. 3.24b) for a limited time in the later fifth century (Konuk 2002, nos. 483–87).

The staggering variety of allied coinages is on display further in this region. Some cities employed the Persian standard, among them the drachma-sized issues of Ionian Erythrai and Kolophon (Fig. 3.25a,b) and the distant polis of Phaselis (Fig. 3.26c) on the southern, Lycian coast of Asia Minor. This city was a great merchant maritime center that did not join the Athenian alliance until the 460s, at the time of the nearby battle of Eurymedon when the Athenians and League members wiped out the Persian navy. The more prevalent standard in the southeastern Aegean was the

a.   b.

c.

Figure 3.25 Other silver civic coins of Ionia, all of the mid-fifth century BC.
(a) Persian-weight drachma of **Erythrai** showing a nude athlete preparing to leap on
a cantering horse; on the reverse a rosette. 4.54 g. *ANS*. (b) Persian-weight drachma
of **Kolophon**, with the head and lyre of Apollo, whose renowned oracle at Klaros
was near the city. 5.38 g. *ANS*. (c) Aeginetan-weight stater of **Teos**, with the state
badge of a griffin facing to the right, and the abbreviated ethnic in letters running
counterclockwise: T-H-I. 11.58 g. *ANS*.

Aeginetan, the standard of four coinages. These are the more or less continuous stater and small-denomination coinages of Ionian Teos (Fig. 3.25c) and
Karian Kaunos (Fig. 3.26b), the exquisite drachma coinage of Knidos
(Fig. 3.26a), and staters and fractions struck by Kamiros (Fig. 3.27a), one
of the three cities on the large island of Rhodes.

   In the late sixth and early fifth centuries, each of the three Rhodian cities,
Kamiros, Ialysos, and Lindos, coined on a different standard, two of them,
Ialysos and Lindos, on unparalleled standards of their own. When Ialysos
resumed coining at some point later in the century, it was in a series of
fractions on the Attic standard: diobols, obols, and half-obols designed with
the head of Athena on reverses (Fig. 3.27b). The Attic weight of these
fractions implies that the city at that time was probably employing
imported Athenian drachmas and tetradrachms for larger denomination
transactions in the city. But beyond the adoption of the Athenian coin
standard, which is unparalleled elsewhere in the region, these fractions are
the only Rhodian coins that display an image of Athena (or up to that time
of any deity), arguably a further expression of strong rapport with Athens.

   In the most recent survey of Rhodian coinage (Stephanakis-Demetriou
2015, 97–101), the latest coinages struck by Kamiros, Ialysos, and Lindos

Figure 3.26 Silver civic coins of the Karian and Lycian coasts. (**a**) Aeginetan-weight drachma of **Knidos** (*c.* mid-fifth century BC), showing the forepart of a lion; on the reverse, the head of the city goddess, Aphrodite, and, around, the letters K-N-I. 6.06 g. *ANS*. (**b**) Aeginetan-weight stater of **Kaunos** (*c.* 430–410 BC), depicting the winged, messenger goddess Iris, holding a caduceus and wreath; on the reverse, a conical baetyl (an aniconic stone image of a divinity, probably the same divinity depicted naturalistically on the obverse), on each side of which is a bunch of grapes and, above, a triangular letter giving the initial of the city in the Karian alphabet. 11.38 g. *ANS*. (**c**) Persian standard tetrobol of **Phaselis** (*c.* 450 BC), depicting a boar's head prow of a ship on the obverse and, on the reverse, a ship's up-curved stern and the abbreviated ethnic Φ-Α-Σ. 3.37 g. *ANS*.

Figure 3.27 Silver coins of Rhodes. (**a**) Aeginetan-weight stater of **Kamiros** (second quarter of fifth century BC) with obverse type of a fig leaf and a reverse of a divided incuse square. 12.04 g. *ANS*. (**b**) Attic-weight diobol of **Ialysos** (probably mid-fifth century to 411 BC): forepart of a winged boar on the obverse; the helmeted head of Athena on the reverse. 1.39 g. *Oxford*.

are persuasively dated to right after 411, when the cities revolted from Athens and allied themselves with Sparta (Thuc. 8.44). The coinages, almost entirely of fractional denominations, were now all of Aeginetan weight and had a common obverse type, the forepart or head of a horse.

The reverse types were badges of the minting cities: the head of a lion for the coins of Lindos (Fig. 3.28a), a rose for Ialysos, and the fig leaf for Kamiros. In 408/7 the cities merged in a single, island-wide state, the polis of Rhodos, which immediately began to mint a long-lasting state coinage on the Chian standard, a standard that at that time was associated with the Spartan war effort (Figs. 3.28b and 7.11d).

We conclude this survey of allied minting by puzzling over one of the most idiosyncratic coinages of fifth-century Greece, the silver stater coinage struck by the island polis of Kos (Fig. 3.29). Produced in three distinct phases between *c.* 480 and 450, it was restricted to a single denomination, either a triple siglos of Persian weight or a light version of Attic tetradrachm weight. Its obverse design is no less exceptional: the discus-thrower and tripod refer to a regional athletic festival of Triopian Apollo at which tripods

a.   b.

Figure 3.28 Silver coins of Rhodes after the island sided with Sparta against Athens. (**a**) Aeginetan-weight diobol of Lindos (411–408/7 BC) showing the forepart of a horse on the obverse and the head of a lion on the reverse. 2.28 g. ANS. (**b**) Chian-weight tetradrachm of the unified state of Rhodes, having a three-quarters facing head of Helios on the obverse and on the reverse the state emblem of a rose (in Greek, rhodon), the ethnic POΔION ("Rhodian"), and the minting magistrate's symbol of an eagle. The symbol identifies the specific issue, one of the first to be struck when the state was formed in 408/7. 15.15 g. Oxford.

Figure 3.29 Stater of Kos (second quarter of fifth century BC), displaying on the obverse a nude athlete preparing to hurl a discus, between a tripod on the left and the legend KOΣ on the right. The crab on the reverse is the state emblem of Kos. 16.12 g. ANS. Usually identified as a triple siglos (Barron 1968; Davis and Sheedy 2019, 17–20), the Koan stater has also been recognized as a light Attic tetradrachm (p. 149).

were awarded as prizes (Hdt. 1.144). Although Kos was one of the five Doric cities that participated in the games, Triopion was in the territory of Knidos, across the strait from Kos. Why then was the festival given prominence on Koan coins? To initially commemorate a Koan victor in the games? Or had the Koans appropriated the festival as their own? Did the staters serve as coinage for the festival, even if there were no smaller denominations to accompany them? Before striking these coins, Kos had minted staters and fractions on the Aeginetan standard (Stephanaki [2012], 445–452); five of these fractions (1.55–1.80 g) in the large Elmalı hoard imply that these continued in use into the 460s, leaving us to wonder all the more why the curious shift to a new standard for the staters with the type of an athlete.

Allied Minting and Athens

There is much still to be learned about these allied coinages individually. But when we take them up as a whole, as in the conspectus presented in Table 3.1, three trends in local minting under the *arche* emerge with some clarity. The first was a discontinuation of minting during the second quarter of the fifth century by more than half of the forty-three allied states that had been striking a coinage of their own around the time that the Athenian alliance was formed. As seen in the numerous coinages of Category *B/b* in Table 3.1, the closing of civic mints during this time included all of those in close proximity to Athens – the Island District – but was by no means limited to them.

Secondly, over time this early decline was counterbalanced by the twenty Category *c* cities that minted for the first time around but mostly after the middle of the century, plus the six Category *B+c* cities that resumed coining in the later fifth century after a long stoppage. In terms of simple totals, in other words, the number of minting allies during the earliest years of the *arche* and the number of cities that were minting *c.* 420–412 BC (i.e., before the empire began to unravel following the disastrous Sicilian expedition) was roughly the same.

Nevertheless – and this is the third and most significant trend – the overall character of local minting had changed through a general decline in the minting of large, stater-size denominations such as were customarily employed in major monetary transactions and transfers. Noticeable already in the second quarter of the century in some Category *B* coinages before they came to an end altogether, minting exclusively in smaller

Table 3.1 *Conspectus of allied coinage*

The cities are listed according to the five administrative districts of the empire and in order of the sums paid in tribute in the late 440s BC (as compiled and discussed by Nixon and Price 1990, 140–150, 166–170). Asterisks denote cities with coins illustrated in the present book.

Letters in parentheses identify the broad temporal category of each city's minting: (A or a) continuous or intermittent minting over the full duration of the city's membership in the *arche*, (B or b) minting that lasted only into the 460s or 450s, and (C or c) minting that did not begin until around or after the middle of the century. Capital letters designate coinages that include large stater-size coins along with smaller denominations. Letters in lowercase indicate smaller-denomination coinages with no unit larger than an Aeginetian drachma (c. 6 g); nearly all coinages beginning in the second half of the century are of this type (c). The designation (B +c) is used for several cities that ceased minting in the second quarter of the century but after a gap of some decades turned to coining again but only in small denominations.

In general, the tribute quotas were based on a city's relative economic resources, often with additional considerations. For instance, the exceptional thirty-talent payments of Thasos and Aegina must have included large installments of reparations for the thousands of talents that Athens had expended in besieging them.

I. ISLAND DISTRICT
Talents

30	Aegina* (pp. 75–7: minting as ally c. 456–431 BC)
18	Paros* (*b*)
6⅔	Naxos* (*B*)
5	Karystos* (*B*)
4	Keos island with two (*B*) cities: Karthaia and Koressos
3	Eretria* (*B*), Chalkis* (*B*), Siphnos* (*B*), Kythnos* (*b*)

II. THRACEWARD DISTRICT

30	Thasos* (*A*)
15	Abdera* (*A*)
10	Ainos* (*C*) beginning to coin c. 460
9	Mende* (*A*)
6	Poteidaia* (*b*), Skione* (*B*), Terone* (*B* +c?), Samothrace* (*b*)

Table 3.1 (*cont.*)

3	Akanthos* (*A*), Aineia* (*c*)
2	Olynthos* (*c*)
1½	Maroneia* (*A*)
1	Aphytis* (*c*)

less than 1: Neapolis* (*B*), Dikaia* (*B*)

III. HELLESPONTINE DISTRICT

12	Lampsakos* (*A*) electrum + (*b?*) silver
9	Kyzikos* (*A*) electrum +(*a*) silver, Kalchedon* (*c*)
5	Selymbria* (*b* +*c*)
4	Abydos* (*b*)
3	Kebren* (*a*), Tenedos* (*B* +*c*), Prokonnesos (*c*)
1	Skepsis* (*a*), Dardanos (*c*)

less than 1: Parion* (*b*), Astakos (*a*), Lamponeia* [p. 97] (*b* +*c*), Neandria* (*c*)

Non-tributary: Mytilene* (*A*): electrum + billon, silver.
Methymna* (*B* +*c*)

No recorded tribute after becoming tributary allies in 427 BC
(pp. 94–5):
Pordoselene* (*c*), Antandros* (*c*), Larisa in Troad* (*c*).

IV. IONIAN DISTRICT

9	Kyme (*c*)
7	Erythrai *(*b*)
6	Ephesos* (*A/a*), Teos* (*A*),
5	Miletos* (*c*)
2	Phokaia* (*A*) electrum
1½	Klazomenai (*b*), Kolophon* (*c*)
1	Assos* (*a*), Myrina (*c*)

less than 1: Gargara* [p. 97] (*c*), Elaia (*c*), Pitane (*c*)

Non-tributary: Samos* (*A*), Chios* (*A*)

V. KARIAN DISTRICT

6	Kamiros* (*B*), Lindos (*B?*), Ialysos* [so: Ialysos*] (*c*), Kos* (*B*),
3	Knidos* (*a*), Phaselis* (*c*)
1⅔	Halikarnassos (*c*)
1½	Astypalia (*b*)

less than 1: Kaunos* (*A*), Idyma (*c*)

denominations had become virtually a rule for new coinages after *c.* 450. The pronounced shift to small denominations occurs even at Mende, which after 424 minted in no silver denomination larger than a *hekte*. By the last decade of the fifth century (by which time Akanthos, Chios, and Ephesos had become independent of Athens), only four to six of the cities allied with Athens were still coining staters or tetradrachms: three or four cities along the eastern coast of Thrace – Thasos, Abdera, Maroneia, and possibly Ainos, all with trading interests in the Balkan hinterlands beyond the *arche* – and Samos and possibly Teos in Ionia. Otherwise, local allied minting had become limited to drachmas, *hektai*, and their fractions.

The closing of civic mints was hardly a new phenomenon. Several allied cities, including Stageira and Sermylia in the Chalkidike, and Ioulis and Thera in the Cyclades, had coined in the late sixth or very early fifth centuries but had stopped by *c.* 480. But what we witness in the early decades of the Athenian alliance is an unmatched acceleration of mint closings, and when this is paired with the orientation of local minting away from the production of large denominations, we find a pattern that runs precisely counter to the relentlessly increasing production and circulation of Athenian coinage, which outside of Attica circulated almost exclusively in high-value tetradrachms. Inasmuch as these opposing monetary dynamics were evidently linked, it follows that the tremendous growth in the availability and use of Athenian tetradrachms was chiefly responsible for the changed profile of the allied coinages.

How else might these changes be explained? With respect to the Cyclades, one commentator has proposed that the local reductions in coining resulted at least in part from an impoverishment of the cities under Athenian domination (Sheedy 2006, 125). This hypothesis of economic decline, however, is not supported by other kinds of material evidence (Osborne 1999; Rutishauser 2012, 115), even if it does seem reasonable to assume that in assembling annual payments of tribute to Athens, some cities might gradually have exhausted any accumulated reserves of silver that would otherwise have been available for coining (Konuk 2011, 66).

Granted that known finds of Attic tetradrachms within the *arche* or near to it are limited to Eretria in Euboea and Methone on the Macedonian coast (Appendix B, nos. 6–8, 37), there is nevertheless indirect evidence for their presence in other local economies. In Siphnos the post-480 introduction of a new denomination (an Aeginetan tetrobol = Attic hemidrachm) implies that Attic-weight coinage had come to circulate alongside the island's traditional coinage of Aeginetan weight (p. 51). And, as we have seen at Ialysos on the island of Rhodes (p. 64) and will see again at Mytilene and in the Troad after Mytilene's failed revolt in 427 (pp. 95–6), new local coinages sprang up, all in small denominations of Attic weight, a very peculiar standard for these regions unless the coins were to be the local components of a larger system involving Athenian money.

In this connection it seems unnecessary to assume that Athens must have decreed early on that its coinage had to be accepted as legal tender in all the cities of the *arche*. Growth in the acceptance of Attic tetradrachms at the expense of local large-value coins could very well have developed on its own. Attic coinage was the coinage of the hegemon as well as the major commercial coinage of the *arche* by virtue of its volume alone; and it was probably in the interest of the cities and bankers to amass it and of merchants and customs officials to accept it. Whether or not it was the required specie for fulfilling financial obligations to Athens, it must certainly have been the preferred one, as presumably it was becoming in interstate trade. And once an allied city allowed Attic money to be accepted along with its local currency, the city could no longer maintain the monopolistic control that had allowed it to profit from the overvaluation and mandatory exchange of a coinage of its own (Kagan 2008, 109). No longer an economic benefit to individual cities, minting could become too expensive and be readily abandoned, except in the case of the smaller denominations, which were not forthcoming from Athens and yet were essential for everyday market transactions and the petty taxes that accompanied many market activities.

The impact of the immense coinage of Alexander the Great on the Greek civic coinages of western Asia Minor in the late fourth and early third centuries BC offers some illustrative parallels. Prior to Alexander's conquest, these civic coinages were flourishing (Meadows 2011, 284–285; Thonemann 2015, 46). But the flood of new coinage that Alexander struck from the massive stores of silver and gold he captured from the royal Persian treasuries was far greater than the fifth-century owl silver of Athens. And one result of its dispersal in the Eastern Greek world was that, as Meadows (2014, 183) has written, "for a century or more after Alexander there was very little locally-produced coinage." It is currently recognized that this shrinkage of minting was not imposed upon the cities by Alexander and the Macedonian kings who followed him but was rather the unintended consequence of the vastness of the Alexander coinage and its obvious convenience as an international all-purpose currency that made the minting of local coinages superfluous and not worth the cost (Martin 1985, 128;

Thonemann 2015, 49). Nevertheless, in the third century BC several Ionian cities like Miletos employed a dual-currency system: while striking a local coinage on a local weight standard for routine, internal buying and selling, these cities held a substantial supply of Attic-weight tetradrachms of Alexander and his successors for the payment of taxes to the ruling power and for other large external transactions that required this kind of internationally accepted money (Marcellesi 2000; Thonemann 2015, 55).

Such interactions between a massive imperial currency and secondary, civic ones correspond closely to what we find in Athens' *arche*, although ultimately the Athenians did formulate a deliberate policy of mandating the adoption of their own coinage. By *c.* 414 they issued a decree that required the use of Athenian coinage along with Athenian weights and measures throughout the empire. We will take up this decree in Chapter 6, while observing here that progress toward the end result envisaged by the decree had already been long in the making.

This survey of allied coinages cannot in many respects be chronologically exact. As readers will have noted, we have often used "before *c.* 450" or the like, a reflection of the difficulty of determining precisely when numismatic changes occurred. Now we turn from this survey to coinages that can be more precisely understood because they correlate with historical events.

4

Numismatic Narratives in the Pentekontaetia, 479–431 BC

The preceding chapter touched on three critical events in the *Pentekontaetia*, the period of nearly fifty years between the defeat of the Persians in 479 BC and the beginning of Peloponnesian War in 431. These were the revolts, first, of Naxos around the year 470, the second of Thasos in the mid-460s, and, finally, that of Samos in 441–440. Athens' suppression of each of these uprisings left its mark in the cities' coinages – at Naxos minting ceased; at Thasos and Samos it was halted, only to resume later. The linkage between these political events and breaks in the coins' chronologies is derived from various numismatic factors, including the evidence of hoards. In this chapter we turn to five other developments in this period in which coins enhance the written historical sources with substantial detail.

The Coinage of Themistokles, His Son, and Grandson(?) at Magnesia, after *c.* 465 BC

The first development of especial interest concerns the extraordinary late career of the Athenian politician and general Themistokles, a key figure in the construction of Athens' navy and in the resistance to Xerxes at the battle of Salamis. He was ostracized from Athens in 472 or 471 and lived the rest of his life in exile, ending up, in 465, at the court of the newly installed Persian King Artaxerxes I, who granted him governorship of the Ionian Greek city Magnesia on the Maeander (in return for his promising to assist the King in his effort to conquer Greece). With this bequest Themistokles received income from the taxes of Magnesia, which came to fifty talents annually, and from two other Greek cities, Myous, also in Ionia, and Lampsakos on the Hellespont (Thuc. 1.138.5) – although whether the King controlled Lampsakos at that time, or just claimed to control it, is uncertain.

Since ancient biographies tended to mythologize the lives of important individuals, the silver coins minted at Magnesia and signed by Themistokles (Fig. 4.1a–c) confirm his rule of the city and his commitment to profit from it. But perhaps of even greater historical interest are the coins minted and signed by his son, Archepolis (Fig. 4.2), after Themistokles' death in

a.   b.   c.

Figure 4.1 Silver coins of **Themistokles** at Magnesia (*c.* 465–459 BC). Attic standard. (**a**) Didrachm depicting Apollo holding a laurel branch staff on the obverse; inscribed (upward at left and downwards at right) ΘΕΜΙΣΤΟΚ-ΛΕΟΣ ("of Themistokles"). On the reverse, an eagle and the letters M-A (for Magnesia). 8.50 g. *Paris*. (**b**) Quarter drachma with the head of Zeus and the letters A-[M] on the obverse; the reverse shows the monogram ΘΕ (for Themistokles). 0.96 g. *Munich*. (**c**) Quarter obol with an owl on the obverse and the same ΘΕ monogram on the reverse. 0.17 g. *CNG*. A didrachm of this coinage in the British Museum is made of bronze covered with thin veneer of silver (Seltman 1933, 108n, pl. XV.14). Such a piece is normally assumed to be the work of a private forger; but given Themistokles' putative reputation for deception, here one cannot be sure.

X 2

Figure 4.2 Silver hemidrachm of **Archepolis** at Magnesia (after 459 BC). Attic standard. On the obverse, Zeus holds a thunderbolt and a long scepter; inscribed ΑΡΧΕ-ΠΟΛΙΣ. On the reverse, an eagle and ligatures containing the letters AP-XE. 2.26 g. *Munich*.

c. 459, which attest to the continuation of family rule in keeping with Persian royal practice of awarding cities to individuals and their offspring in return for loyalty to the regime.

These coins were all minted on the Attic standard and with their plethora of small fractions were clearly meant for internal circulation. The seven denominations (Nollé and Wenninger 1998/1999; Sheedy 2017) range from didrachm-staters (8.6 g) down to quarters of an obol (0.17 g) and (in the series of Archepolis) even tiny eighths of an obol (0.08 g), the smallest unit ever minted in an extant Greek silver coinage. The choice of standard is notable, for at this time the Attic standard and denominational system were rarely employed outside of Athens. Like this weight standard, the owl reverse type of Themistokles' quarter-obol (Fig. 4.1c) also looks back to Athens. On the larger denominations Themistokles' name is fully spelled out in the genitive case on the obverse, implying that these were coins *of* Themistokles, whereas the city of Magnesia is named only in the two-letter abbreviation M-A on the reverse. On the smaller coins of Themistokles his two-letter ΘE monogram makes up the entire reverse type. Such association of the coinage with the authority of a ruler is decidedly auto-cratic, as is the fact that, as mentioned, Themistokles was able to pass on his authority to his son in a dynastic succession characteristic of Greek tyrants and several other petty Greek rulers in Persian western Asia Minor (Nollé and Wenninger 1998/1999, 46–52). How long Archepolis remained in power is unknown. His extant coins are signed with his name or an abbreviation of it in ligatures; the majority of the coins (like the one pictured in Fig. 4.2) lack any letters referring to Magnesia at all.

In his survey of these dynastic coinages of Magnesia, Kenneth Sheedy (2017) has added a third phase of later fifth-century obols and fractions of the obol, some of which are stamped with the familiar ΘE monogram of Themistokles. These he attributes to a presumed younger Themistokles, who would have taken his name and monogram from his grandfather and extended the family rule of Magnesia for a generation after Archepolis. These petty rulers who owed their authority to the favor of the Persian king typically were free to mint a local coinage that was entirely independent, in both visual content and metrology, of the Great King's own royal money. Monopolistic control of coinage was not a concern of the Persian monarchy. The kings minted their own gold coinage of darics, and, in western Asia Minor, a silver coinage of sigloi (Fig. 7.1a,b), and spent them lavishly, especially in subsidiz-ing opposition to Athens in the concluding phases of the Peloponnesian War. Even so, Persian officials also employed Athenian coinage when convenient, minted imitations of it (Fig. 2.11), and were generally content to let their Greek subjects coin locally as they chose (Le Rider 2001, 186).

Subjugation of Aegina, 457 BC

The famous turtle staters of Aegina, the wealthy island polis that lay in sight of Athens directly across the Saronic Gulf, were the most prolific silver coinage in the fifth-century Aegean after the owl tetradrachms of Athens. Like Attic tetradrachms, they had been minted on a lavish scale since the sixth century; and while they and their fractional divisions were an important element of the local, maritime-based Aeginetan economy, the staters were

a.   b.

Figure 4.3 Silver staters of **Aegina,** both with "skewed" divisions in the large incuse square on the reverse. Aeginetan standard. (**a**) Obverse of a turtle with T-shaped pattern of dots on its shell (*c.* 470s–457 BC). 12.32 g. *ANS.* (**b**) Tortoise with segmented shell (*c.* 456–431 BC). 12.15 g. *ANS.*

exported in quantity and circulated internationally from the Cyclades to Crete, throughout nearly the whole of the Peloponnesus, and up into central Greece as far as Thessaly in a zone that stood mostly outside of Athens' *arche*, as did Doric Aegina itself – until 457. In that year Athens, after defeating the Aeginetans at sea and a long siege,, forced them to tear down their walls, give up their warships, and become subject to the Athenians (Thuc. 1.105.2, 108.4), paying a severe tribute of thirty talents annually. One might expect that upon capturing Aegina the Athenians would have used this opportunity to shut down the mint of this popular coinage of one of their bitterest rivals. Instead, after a presumed break, Aegina continued to coin, although with a conspicuous modification of the obverse type.

From the archaic beginnings of the coinage, around the middle of the sixth century, a simple sea turtle appears on the obverse, an appropriate-enough badge for this island with its famed merchant fleet (Fig. 4.2a), although this need not be why the type was initially chosen. In modern Greek an ingot is called a "turtle" (*chelona*), an association that very well may go back to antiquity when small, poured ingots of silver commonly had a roughly hemispherical, turtle-like shape. It has been proposed that if early Aeginetan traders in silver did refer to their small ingots as "turtles," when they began to stamp the silver out as coins they added the turtle symbol as a kind of pun (Kroll 2008, 36n; Sheedy 2012, 106).

In the course of the fifth century, the sea turtle was replaced on the coins by a terrestrial tortoise with a segmented shell (Fig. 4.2b). Hoards and the overstriking of some of these tortoise coins by Azbaal of Kition, a Cypriot king of the third quarter of the fifth century (Kraay 1976, 306), indicate that this change occurred around the middle of the century and strongly suggests that it was a consequence of Athens' capture of Aegina in 457. Moreover, from the uneven shapes and layered thicknesses of the flans of the new tortoise coins, it is clear that the change of type had a functional, economic purpose. Their sandwiched, irregular flans together with the elemental composition of their silver, which is identical to that of the preceding turtle coins, show that the tortoise coins were minted over the turtle coins, which had been hammered flat and then folded over before restriking.

From written sources and the reminting of Athens' owl coinage with a modified type in the middle of the fourth century (Kroll 2011a), we know that Greek states in need of money could raise revenue by declaring their existing coinage invalid as legal tender, which then had to be recalled for restriking with a different type; upon restriking, the new coinage was returned to their previous owners with a certain number of coins deducted as an exchange or minting fee (in effect a tax), which the state pocketed as profit. This is apparently what the Aeginetans did with their coinage soon after 457. Having suffered a crushing defeat, and facing the recurring financial demands of Athenian tribute, they turned to their coinage as a source of revenue (Kroll 2017, 380; Picard 1978). If, as it seems, the reminting was an Aeginetan initiative, the design of the changed type ought to have been a decision of the Aeginetans as well. For some scholars (e.g., Sheedy 2012, 108) the decision was simply to distinguish the new coins from the old. We would not be amiss, however, to seek a symbolic, political element to the particular design chosen. Was this land tortoise intended to connote a weakened Aegina that had lost its power at sea (as might have been chosen by a collaborationist regime seeking to ingratiate itself with Athens)? Alternatively, might it have been a statement of resilience, or even defiance by a state that still maintained its land and commercial strength?

In any event, the long-standing hostility between Aegina and Athens was never extinguished, and in 431, the first year of the Peloponnesian War, Athens expelled the Aeginetans from their island and settled Athenians there in their place. Perhaps the Aeginetans continued the reminting of old turtle staters in the sites of their exile. Later hoards and evidence like the distant overstriking of the coins on Cyprus, mentioned earlier, confirm that large numbers of the restruck staters were drawn into external circulation, continuing the outflow that had characterized the spread and demand for Aeginetan coinage since its beginning. As an expression of Athens' attitude toward the coining of money by the members of its *arche*, the Aeginetan restriking, no matter how interpreted, provides a good indication that, at least down to the middle of the fifth century, member cities of the Athenian *arche* were free to mint, or not, as they chose.

Thracian and Macedonian Coinage and Athens' Advances in the North, 476–437 BC

In the Aegean world of the fifth century BC, the most prolific source of precious metal outside of the Laureion mining district of Attica was to be found in Thrace, in the vicinity of Mt. Pangaion between the Strymon river and the mainland opposite the island of Thasos. Initially, the mines of this extensive area were worked by local Thracian tribes, whose character- istically large and ostentatious silver coins, which seem to have been mostly minted for export, attest to the great mineral wealth of the region. As their chronology has become better understood, these coins have come also to provide important evidence for reconstructing the competition for access to this wealth by three outside powers: the Parians and Thasians, King Alexander I of Macedon, and Athenians.

The coinage of the Thracian Edonians, who occupied territory along the east bank of the lower Strymon, was signed by their (otherwise unknown) King Getas (Fig. 4.4). By far the most abundant of the tribal coinages, however, was the coinage of the Bisaltians (p. 10), the Thracians inhabiting the lands to the west of the river. Displaying an unmounted horseman, their coinage began in the 470s, after the Persians had been expelled from the area, and continued on into the next decade. The inscribed coins (Fig. 4.5), well represented in the Emalı hoard (Appendix B, no. 41), were followed by a large group without the inscribed ethnic that predominates in the later Carchemish hoard (Appendix B, no. 44). Some coins in both groups

Figure 4.4 Silver tristater of **Getas**, king of the Edonians (460s BC). Parian-Thasian standard. The obverse depicts a nude, bearded herdsman wearing hat with a brim and driving two oxen; inscribed ΝΟΜ-ΙΣ-ΜΑ ΕΔΟΝΕΟΝ ΒΑΣΙΛ-ΕΟΣ ΓΙΤΑ ("Coin of Getas, King of the Edonians"); a wheel is shown on the reverse. 29.07 g. *Lanz 155 (2011)*. Getas is known only from his coins.

Figure 4.5 Silver tristater of the **Bisaltians** (470s–460s BC). Parian-Thasian standard. The nude horseman on the obverse, wearing a hat with brim, carrying two spears, and walking next to his horse is a Thracian divinity or hero. The ethnic ΒΙΣΑ-ΛΤΙΚΩΝ ("of the Bisaltians") is rendered in letters (some inverted) of the Parian-Thasian alphabet, in which the letter *beta* is represented as a "C." 28.68 g. *CNG Triton 18 (2015) 427.*

Figure 4.6 Silver tristater of the **Bisaltians** (460s BC). Parian-Thasian standard with same obverse type as in Fig. 4.5, although horse is branded on the flank with a caduceus symbol, and there is no inscribed ethnic. 27.29 g. *Lanz 159 (2014) 82.*

were struck with the same reverse die (Brackmann 2015), and some of the uninscribed coins introduce the detail of a caduceus branded on the flank of the horse (Fig. 4.6). Subsequently, the coinage was imitated by Alexander I, who added his name around the four-part square on reverses and adopted not only the horseman type but even on certain obverse dies the detail of the caduceus brand (Fig. 4.7). This same brand appears again on the horses portrayed on coins of the later Macedonian king, Pausanias (393 BC; *BMC Macedonia*, 169).

According to Herodotos (5.17), Alexander possessed a mine that produced a talent of silver a day and was situated, outside of Macedonia proper, across Mt. Dysoron at Lake Prasias. The location of this mountain, lake, and mine has been a matter of dispute (Archibald 2013, 66–7; Hammond 1997), but here is where the coins come into play; for the continuation of the

Figure 4.7 Silver tristater of **Alexander I** (*c.* 463 to 454 BC). Parian-Thasian standard. Similar obverse type with caduceus brand but in an advanced style; the horseman also wears a cloak, and there is a crescent symbol behind his head. The inscription around the square on the reverse reads ΑΛΕ-ΧΑ-ΝΔ-ΡΟ ("of Alexander"). 28.7 g. *Baldwins N.Y. Sale 27 (2012) 292.*

Bisaltian-type tristaters by Alexander implies that the mine and the lake were in Bisaltia and that Alexander may have taken possession of the mine by extending his territory as far as the lake on the Strymon River. With his death around 453, his son and successor, Perdikkas II, was unable to hold onto the territory, and probably because of the loss of the mine with it, royal Macedonian minting was suspended for about twenty years.

As noted earlier, other contenders for the resources of the Strymon included the islanders of Paros and its colony Thasos. In the sixth century they established a string of commercial harbors (*emporia*) along the coast opposite Thasos from Neapolis to the Strymon, with the strategic city of Eïon at the mouth of the Strymon as the western limit. They also settled Berge, some twenty-three miles up the river, apparently as an *emporion* for the Thracian river trade. The early influence of the Parians and Thasians in the region is documented in the Parian-Thasian lettering and the weight standard of the Thracian tribal coins.

Athenians also knew well the metallic riches to be had in this region. In the mid-sixth century, Peisistratos came to the Strymon in search of revenue to fund his aspirations to become tyrant of Athens (and also participated in a colonial venture in the Chalkidike). Awareness of the riches helps to explain the Athenians' conquest of Eïon under the command of Kimon, upon gaining the leadership of the Delian League. The site had been taken over by the Persians when they gained control of Macedonia, and it served as a major stronghold and their supply depot for Xerxes' land and sea forces en route to Greece from Asia. After removing them, the Athenians established Eïon and its territory as an Athenian colony and

Figure 4.8 Silver *hemihekte* of **Eïon** (fifth century BC). Parian-Thasian standard. Although this coinage with the types of a waterbird and a lizard overhead (creatures of the marshy Strymon delta) originated before 480 BC when Eïon was still a Parian-Thasian polis under Persian domination, it continued to be minted well down into the fifth century, probably as a multistandard fraction for larger denominations brought to the Athenian *emporion* in trade. The tiny letter eta (H) to the left of the bird's legs should be the city's initial. 0.87 g. *ANS*.

emporion (Fig. 4.8). It also served as a fortified naval station for attempts to gain control of the Strymon corridor. The Athenians' interest in profiting directly from mines as well as *emporia* soon became even more explicit when they tried to wrest these from the Thasians, which led the Thasians to revolt. But after a two-year siege the Athenians under Kimon's command forced Thasos to submit and relinquish its claim to the mining and commercial control of the Thracian littoral. Upon returning to Athens, Kimon was accused (but later acquitted) of accepting a bribe from Alexander I for not going further after territory claimed by Macedon (Plut. *Kimon* 14.2); this anecdote suggests that Kimon may have initially considered contesting Alexander's occupation of Bisaltia (Kagan 1987, 24).

What is certain is that with competition from Thasos and Alexander I eliminated, the Athenians had a much easier time achieving their long-term ambitions in the lower Strymon valley. From the Athenian Tribute Quota lists we learn that two Greek cities on the Strymon were brought into the Athenian alliance in 452 and 451: Argilos opposite Eïon at the mouth of the river and, upriver, the Thasian foundation of Berge, mentioned earlier. Around 447 Perikles sent a large number colonists to settle "among the Bisaltians" (Plut. *Per.* 11.5). Near the middle of the century, too, the last of the Thracian tribal coinages came to an end. Since it is unlikely that all of the mines around Mt. Pangaion suddenly stopped producing, one suspects that their silver was henceforth being exported by Greek middlemen, with the Athenians especially well placed to take advantage. Or perhaps the rights to many of the mines themselves passed into Athenian hands. In any event, since Athenian minting underwent a great expansion around this time (p. 20), it is conceivable that access to Thracian silver may have played a significant part (Wartenberg 2015, 360–1).

In 437/436 the Athenians returned to the site of the Nine Ways, a short distance from the mouth of the Strymon (they had attempted to settle the site since the 460s and even to venture further into the hinterland), refounded it as Amphipolis, and finally gained firm control of the Strymon traffic, with its wealth in metals and shipbuilding timber. Several fifth-century Athenian silver fractions (a triobol, obols, and hemiobols) found in the area and now on display in the Amphipolis museum were most likely brought there by Athenian colonists. Athens' success in the Strymon region, however, was relatively short lived. As detailed in the next chapter, the Athenians lost not only the colony of Amphipolis but also a number of tributary subjects in the Chalkidike during the first phase of the Peloponnesian War.

The Coinage of Corinth's War with Corcyra, 435–433 BC

In his account of the grievances and conflicts that directly led to the outbreak of the Peloponnesian War, Thucydides narrates at some length a sequence of events of the second half of the 430s in which Corinth was centrally involved and into which Athens was drawn (Thuc. 1.26–55).

The events began at the city of Epidamnos (Roman Dyrrachium), in what is now Albania; the city was a colony of the large island of Corcyra to the south. Corcyra was a major sea power and itself a colony of Corinth, which contributed a founder (*oikist*) to Epidamnos. Colonial relationships involved various expected, if unwritten, obligations, to assist at times of need, to pay honor to the mother city (e.g., at festivals), and generally, to be mutually supporting; failure to do so was not considered a minor offence. The relationship between Corinth and Corcyra, however, was decidedly hostile. These details provide the backdrop for understanding the critical unfolding of events at this time that led to war. Let's return to Epidamnos, which was in the midst of civil war. Upon appeal to Corcyra, the mother city refused to help, so the Epidamnians – on the advice of the Delphic oracle – turned to Corinth. The Corinthians readily accepted the Epidamnians' request in large part because of their animosity toward Corcyra. But when the Corcyreans found out, in retaliation, they besieged Epidamnos; in turn, the Corinthians prepared a new colonial expedition and military force to relieve the Epidamnians.

What was now a war between Corinth and Corcyra moved to the south, where a naval battle took place near Corcyra off Cape Leukimme, which the Corcyreans won. This was in 435. The Corinthians then spent two years rounding up allies not only from the Peloponnese but from all over Greece. News of the Corinthians' preparations alarmed the Corcyreans; lacking a powerful ally, they were able to persuade Athens to make a purely defensive alliance with them, the most the Athenians would offer out of concern to respect one term of the Thirty Years Peace with Sparta according to which neither side could fight a member of the other's alliance. But at the battle of Sybota, Corinthian and Athenian ships did indeed come into contact, constituting grounds, according to Corinth, for charging Athens with breaking the Peace.

The theater of conflict and retaliation now centered on a different colonial relationship to the east, in the Chalkidike. Poteidaia was a Corinthian colony but also a subject of Athens; it also, remarkably, had a Corinthian magistrate. The Athenians suspected that the Corinthians would urge their colonists to revolt and so told the Poteidaians to order the magistrate to leave, to raze their walls, and to give hostages. But the city did revolt, and Athens began a costly siege, some 2,000 talents by the time it ended in 429 (Thuc. 2.70, with 2.13.3). Thanks to the meticulous studies of Colin Kraay (1979) and Jonathan Kagan (1998; 2013) it is now possible to see the significance of coinages in the unfolding of these events. The coinages are those of Corinth and of the string of settlements Corinth founded from the mouth of the Corinthian Gulf to well up the Adriatic coast, as well as, of course, islands like Corcyra. Indeed, without any literary evidence, we could go far toward reconstructing the relationship between the mother city and its colonists by reference to their coinages alone.

Let's begin with Corinth. Ever since the sixth century the city had been striking silver staters with a winged, flying Pegasos and the letter *qoppa* (ϙ, the archaic initial of the city) on obverses and on reverses the helmeted head of a youthful goddess. During a brief period in the 430s, the production of the staters suddenly became intensive and involved the simultaneous use of a multiplicity of obverse and reverse dies, the addition of administrative symbols, and the employment of new die-cutters, hired for the increased output. They introduced a number of stylistic innovations, like a more natural, pointed wing for Pegasos (Fig. 4.10).

Five of Corinth's colonies joined in striking related Corinthian-type staters. The colonial coinages of Ambrakia which marked its Pegasos staters with an *alpha* (Fig. 4.11a), and of Leukas, whose staters are marked with a *lambda* (Fig. 4.11d), were substantial. Two other colonies provided small issues, each from a single pair of dies: Anaktorion (originally Wanaktorion), identified by a *digamma* (Greek *W*) (Fig. 4.11b), and Poteidaia, identified by

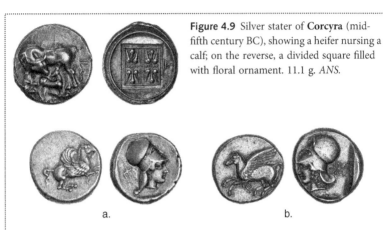

Figure 4.9 Silver stater of **Corcyra** (mid-fifth century BC), showing a heifer nursing a calf; on the reverse, a divided square filled with floral ornament. 11.1 g. *ANS*.

a.   b.

Figure 4.10 Silver staters of **Corinth** (*c.* 436–433 BC), depicting Pegasos with the archaic letter *koppa* below and, on the reverse, the head of a helmeted goddess with an administrative symbol behind. (**a**) with trident symbol. 8.57 g. ANS. (**b**) with palmette symbol, 8.61 g. *ANS*. Innovations in the mass minting of this coinage included the addition of these administrative symbols and on (b) the naturalistic pointed wing of Pegasos, the enlarged, more refined head of the goddess, and the leather neck flap beneath her helmet. Usually identified as Athena, the goddess is more probably the principal state deity of Corinth, Armed Aphrodite, in origin Astarte, the Phoenician goddess of love and war (Blomberg 1996; Smith 2005; Williams 1986, 20).

its initial *pi* (Fig. 4.12). Epidamnos contributed two slight issues, one signed with an *epsilon* and a club symbol beneath the Pegasos, the other with an *epsilon* alone (Fig. 4.11c). These colonial *pegasi* attest to the close bond between Corinth and these cities it founded. Ambrakia, Leukas, and Anaktorion, along with other Corinthian colonies clustered in and around the region of northwestern Greece known collectively as Ambrakia, employed Corinthian and Corinthian-type coins as their established local currency, making the whole region a Corinthian monetary zone.

Corcyra stood apart. Its coinage (Fig. 4.9) was substantial but isolated: it bears no relationship in types or metrology to the coinage of Corinth, nor to the several coinages of Corinth's other colonies in northwestern Greece, nor, for that matter, to any other polis coinages of the region. It was struck to an idiosyncratic stater standard (11.5 g) that decreased over the fifth century to 10.9 g; unsurprisingly, barely any specimens have been found in overseas hoards. The significance of this cannot be overlooked, given the unified monetary, commercial relationship Corinth had with its other colonies in the region.

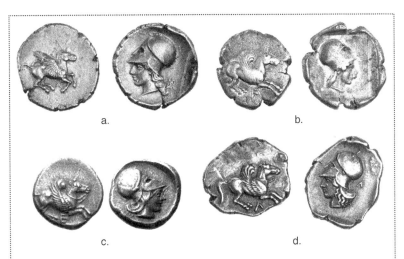

Figure 4.11 Silver staters of Corinthian colonies (*c.* 436–433 BC), similar to the staters of Corinth, but with different identifying city initials beneath Pegasos. (**a**) **Ambrakia**, with initial A, 8.56 g. *ANS.* (**b**) **Anaktorion**, with initial F (*digamma*), 8.17 g. *ANS.* (**c**) **Epidamnos**, with initial E, 8.39 g. *Oxford.* (**d**) **Leukas**, with initial Λ (*lambda*) beneath Pegasos and also on the reverse, behind the head of the goddess, 8.54 g. *ANS.*

Figure 4.12 Corinthian-type stater of **Poteidaia** (*c.* 436–433 BC), with the initial Π (*pi*) behind the head of the goddess. Seated on Pegasos is the hero Bellerophon holding a lowered spear. 8.08 g. *ANS.*

Now in the 430s, with Corinth joined by Epidamnos, Poteidaia, and the three cities in the Ambrakian zone, it is easy to see how this evidently coordinated program of monetary production lends vital detail to Thucydides' accounts of Corinth's preparations for the two naval engagements to rescue Epidamnos from the forces of Corcyra. For the first expedition, in 435, Thucydides (1.27) mentions Corinth's appeals to friendly cities for ships and money. The resulting fleet of seventy-five ships, half from Corinth and half from allied cities including Leukas and Ambrakia, was defeated off Corcyra at Cape Leukimme. As mentioned earlier, preparations for the second and much larger naval effort were extensive (434–433). Thucydides (1.31.1) emphasizes the Corinthians' concentration on the building of ships and the recruiting of rowers from all over Greece with generous financial inducements. Even so, at the Battle of Sybota in 433, this second force of 150 Corinthian, Ambrakian, and allied ships was also unsuccessful, this time with Corcyra's navy supported by some ships from Athens.

A small group of Corinthian and Ambrakiot staters – struck from five and three obverse dies, respectively – belongs stylistically at the beginning of the mass minting and was presumably struck in preparation for the first naval operation. The modest issue of staters from Anaktorion stylistically belongs with this earlier group, as did the first of the two Epidamnian issues that was evidently minted in the city prior to its capture by the Corcyreans in 435. (The later issue was possibly coined by a faction of Epidamnians in exile in support of the 433 expedition.) The main concentration of the Corinthian and colonial minting of Pegasos staters, however, must be attributed to the more ambitious and protracted construction and manning of the second fleet that engaged with Corcyra at Sybota. The volume of this minting makes the point clearly: its production involved twenty-four obverse and thirty-eight reverse dies at Corinth, twelve obverse and twenty-six reverse dies at Ambrakia, and two obverse and seventeen reverse dies at Leukas – altogether an extraordinary record for a mere two years of coining.

Although these two concentrated mintings of Corinthian and allied coinages are by no means the only known ancient instances of coining specifically in preparation for war (Howgego 1990, 7–9), they are among the better documented. In addition, in this group, one of the small Corinthian-type issues adds a crucial piece of evidence for the growing rift between Athens and Corinth. This is the Poteidaian issue signed with a *pi* and designed with the figure of Bellerophon seated on the Pegasos (Fig. 4.12), recalling Poteidaia's earlier coin type of a mounted Poseidon Hippios (Fig. 3.8c). Whether struck for the first Corinthian force in 435 or during the assembling of the larger fleet in 434–433, the issue documents financial assistance to Corinth even while, as a member of the Athenian *arche*, Poteidaia was (presumably – the record is too fragmentary for certainty) annually paying tribute to Athens. Members of the *arche* were free to make donations to whomever they wished; but in 433, after Athens concluded its implicitly anti-Corinthian alliance with Corcyra and sent ships that ultimately contributed to the Corinthian's failure at Sybota, Poteidaia's recent minting of money for the Corinthian cause, if known to the Athenians, could only have strengthened Athens' fears of continued Poteidaian collaboration with Corinth. In any case, in the aftermath of Sybota, as mentioned, Athens ordered the Poteidaians to expel their

Corinthian magistrate, tear down their walls and give hostages, and soon learned that Corinth and King Perdikkas II of Macedon were conspiring to get Poteidaia to revolt (Thuc. 1.56). After it did, the fighting between the Corinthian expeditionary force sent out to reinforce Poteidaia and the much larger contingent dispatched by Athens to besiege it led the Corinthians to call for an assembly of the Peloponnesian League at Sparta to debate the prospect of going to war with Athens.

Thus, we learn much in these episodes about the Corinthians and their animosities, first directed against Corcyra, then Athens, as well as the Athenians' hard-nosed approach to Poteidaia. Both sides were consumed by hatred and the desire for retaliation, which would lead exponentially in scale from these localized colonial hostilities to "global war" between Sparta and its allies and Athens and its empire.

Dionysios Chalkous and the Bronze Coinage of Attic Salamis

One of the most far-reaching innovations in the monetary history of ancient Greece was the adoption of bronze as a monetary metal. The minting of low-value coins in bronze had been pioneered by certain Greek cities of Sicily and Italy around the middle part of the fifth century and solved two major problems with small fractional units of silver: for the states that minted them they were difficult and expensive to strike in quantity, and for users they were inconvenient to handle. Since bronze was a relatively inexpensive metal, fiduciary – that is, highly overvalued – bronze fractional coinages were quite profitable to produce. In the last decade or two of the fifth century, the striking of bronze fractions was taken up by Rhodes (Ashton 2001, 90) and in northern Greece by King Archelaos I of Macedon (413–399 BC), the Chalkidian League, and the cities of Mende and, when resettled as an Athenian cleruchy, Poteidaia (Bresson 2016, 262–3; Gatzolis 2013; Psoma 2001, 143). According to two specimens excavated in the Kerameikos cemetery area in Athens, however, the earliest bronze coins minted in Aegean Greece were those struck by the people of Salamis, the island lying off the western coast of Attica (Fig. 5.14). The archaeological contexts of the two specimens give a starting date for this substantial coinage as early as the 430s BC (Kroll 2013).

Salamis was an anomalous offshore dependency of Athens. Although settled with a cleruchy of Athenian citizens, it also retained a native community that was never incorporated into the Athenian citizen body

Figure 4.13 Bronze coin of Attic **Salamis**, 430s to *c.* 400 BC and later, displaying on the obverse the head of the nymph Salamis and, on the reverse, an oblong shield and on it a sword in a sheath with strap; the letters on each side of the shield give the abbreviated ethnic: ΣΑ-ΛΑ, "(of the) Sala(minians)." This old-fashioned type of shield with cutout sides represents the famous shield of Ajax, the Homeric hero who came from Salamis. The coin probably represents one-quarter of an obol. 3.33 g. *CNG (2002).*

(Hansen 2004). Accordingly, it exercised certain prerogatives of self-rule, of which one was the minting of this bronze coinage that in every respect was independent of the silver owl coinage of Athens.

Ancient references to a prominent Athenian orator and poet facetiously known as Dionysios Chalkous ("Dionysios the Bronze Coin") imply that he got the epithet from his obsession with the advantages of bronze coinage (Athen. 15.669d). He was one of the leaders of the Athenian colonization at Thourioi in southern Italy in 443 (Plut. *Nic.* 5.2; Brousseau 2013, 83) and probably travelled widely in the West. Upon returning to Athens, he tirelessly advocated the adoption of this radically new kind of coinage. While unsuccessful in persuading the Athenians, he may nevertheless have provided the inspiration for the Salaminian bronzes, which circulated not only on the island but, as finds indicate, in and around the rest of Attica. The coins must have fulfilled a need for a more abundant and convenient small change on the island and in the region generally.

It is sometimes suggested that the introduction of base metal coins in northern Greece was a response to the economic pressures of war. This might apply also to the Salaminian bronze if it commenced just as the Peloponnesian War was getting underway. But the start of the coinage appears to have been earlier, and since the practicality of small denomination coinages in bronze was just as great during times of peace, their profitability for the issuer and simple practicality for users were probably motivations enough (Bresson 2016, 269). Over the course of the fourth century, the innovation was embraced by nearly every minting city in the Greek world, with the result that by the end of that century silver obols and fractions of the obol had been replaced by bronze just about everywhere.

5

The Archidamian War, 431–421 BC

Both sides were at their height in every kind of preparedness. This was the greatest upheaval that ever befell not only Greece but also a large part of the barbarian [i.e., non-Greek] world – one might say almost of mankind. (Thuc. 1.1.1–2)

Now we move to the Peloponnesian War, the first ten years of which is known as the Archidamian War, after the Spartan king and general, Archidamos, who led the first invasion of Athens in 431. In the previous chapter we emphasized the role of the Corinthians, a critical Spartan ally, in the events immediately preceding the war's outbreak. Corinth used its clout with the Spartans – considerable, not least, because of Corinth's geographical position at the entry to the Peloponnese, but also because of its wealth and naval power – to garner support for war with Athens, thereby to ensure that the "grievances and disputes" (Thuc. 1.23.5-6) of Peloponnesian League allies translated into a vote for war. We also mentioned Athens' culpability in infringing the terms of the Thirty Years Peace signed in 446 between Sparta and Athens by sending some ships to fight Corinth at Sybota.

Thucydides' claim about the "greatest upheaval" at the opening of his work was largely founded on the resources that each side possessed. But it turns out that Thucydides is speaking of two very different sources of power:

The Spartan hegemony did not involve the imposition of tribute, but they took care to ensure oligarchic rule exclusively in their own interest; whereas the Athenians in time came to deprive all subject cities of their ships and require payment of tribute, with the exceptions of Chios and Lesbos. (Thuc. 1.19, trans. Hammond)

This pithy synopsis of the different bases of Athens' and Sparta's power speaks to their respective spheres of military supremacy, one on sea and the other on land. It neatly underscores our observation in Chapter 1 about the distinctiveness of naval power compared to land power. Thucydides highlights the difference by including a speech for Archidamos that makes clear that the Spartan king, particularly, gets that. In an assembly of Spartans to deal with the conflict with Athens and the prospect of war, he argued forcefully that an immediate recourse to war was premature: as Thucydides has him ask – the speeches are not verbatim records – his countrymen: *"What will we fight them with? With ships? We don't have them. With money? We have none in our public treasury! Nor are we ready to contribute it from our private funds"* (Thuc. 1.80.4). He then sums it all up: *"war is not so much a matter of arms, but of expense, through which arms provide an advantage"* (1.83.2). But the Spartan Ephor Sthenelaidas, a proponent of war sooner than later, countered with this: *"[The Athenians] may have money and ships . . . but we have brave men"* (Thuc. 1.86.3). That simple formulation struck a chord, precisely because Sthenelaidas was tapping into the Spartan military psyche: war was a soldier's business, with spear and shield. Sthenelaidas' proposal won.

Let us skip over to Athens. On the eve of war Perikles (who, incidentally, is depicted earlier [Thuc. 1.127.3] as a steadfast Spartan-hater determined to drag his city into war) addressed the Athenians, saying:

> that their strength lay in the revenue from their allies, and that most wars were won by good judgment and abundant financial resources. He urged them to be confident since they had 600 talents coming in annually from the allies, most of it from tribute. This in addition to other revenues; and they had 6,000 talents on the Acropolis in their own coinage. (Thuc. 2.13.3)

He then goes on to list other wealth on the Acropolis, recently centralized from the treasuries of the gods' sanctuaries throughout Attica, now amalgamated for safekeeping once war was imminent, and all usable – in essence these were public funds. The thousands of talents "on the Acropolis" is a way of referring largely to the Treasury of Athena, a kind of reserve bank, out of which coined money could be borrowed and expended (but was expected to be repaid).

These comments provide revealing snapshots of not just the difference between the Athenians' and Spartans' use of money in war but also their different attitudes and perceptions, the polarity best exemplified by Sthenelaidas and Perikles. As Perikles points out, "it is financial reserves that win war, not ad hoc financing" (Thuc. 1.141.5), a principle tested throughout the Peloponnesian War.

Two documents inscribed on stone also illuminate the differences between the war economies. The first, a list of contributions to the Spartan war fund, now surviving in battered fragments, was erected in the Sanctuary of Apollo at Amyklai near Sparta, between *c.* 427 and 407 BC.

> *The (?)Ephesian exiles(?) who are the friends of the Spartans, gave for*
> *the war four hundred darics. . . . The Aeginetans gave to the Spartans*
> *for the war fourteen minas and ten staters. The . . . -oi gave to the*
> *Spartans . . . darics. Som . . . ophon of Olenos in Achaea and Hod- . . .*
> *of Aitolia (?) gave to the Lacedaemonians . . . for the war pay for*
> *triremes (?) and thirty-two minas of silver. The exiled Chians, who are*
> *friends of the Spartans, gave one thousand Aeginetan staters . . . -non*
> *gave to the Spartans for the war four thousand . . . and [four to nine]*
> *thousand other . . . and of raisins . . . talents. The . . . gave . . . many . . .*
> *and eight hundred darics and . . . talents. . . . gave for the war . . . thirty*
> *minas and . . . [two or three] thousand medimnoi (bushels) and [thir-*
> *to nine]ty . . . and sixty. . . . The Ephesians gave to the Spartans for the*
> *war one thousand darics . . .*
>
> *The Melians gave to the Spartans twenty minas of silver. Mol- the Lokrian*
> *(?) gave to the Spartans one talent of silver. The Melians gave to the*
> *Spartans . . .* (O&R 151, with the translation largely followed here)

This inscription says more about the donors' economies than the Spartans',
but it nonetheless highlights the Spartans' fundamentally different
approach to funding the war (out of necessity) versus the Athenians' ability
to draw upon regular monetary income and the build-up of their reserves.
The inscribed document of the "Spartan war fund," replete with nonmo-
netary contributions in bushels of wheat and so many talent weights of
raisins, would be as unthinkable in Athens as it would be to find in Sparta a
stele containing year-after-year monetary receipts to Athena such as are
inscribed on the *Lapis Primus*.

Another invaluable piece of epigraphic evidence speaks directly to coinage in particular as comprising a critical mass of Athens' wealth, and, as in
the case of Perikles' list of financial resources earlier, kept in sacred
treasuries: a decree of the popular assembly that refers to a repayment of
"three thousand talents to Athena in our own coinage":

> *Resolved by the Boule and the People, Kekropis held the prytany,*
> *Mnesitheus was Secretary, Eupeithes presided, Kallias made the*
> *motion. Repayment shall be made to the gods of the moneys that are*
> *owed them, since the three thousand talents, which were voted for*
> *Athena, have been brought up to the Acropolis, in our own coinage . . .*

This small extract from the beginning of the "first Kallias Decree" (O&R
144, *AIO*) highlights the central role of the Athenian assembly – the

sovereign political body of the polis – in managing its (sacred) finances. We noted that the borrowing of such funds housed in sacred treasuries needed to be repaid. This decree attests to such repayment. The decree was probably passed in 431 BC. (Kallet-Marx 1989; Samons 2000, 113–63, 212–48, though see the conventional dating of 434 in O&R) in connection with the preparations for war with Sparta and its allies, when all Athenians dwelling outside the city walls of Athens moved inside with their possessions. Like Perikles' accounting in Thucydides' *History*, the decree denotes financial strength through not only statements of quantity and future replenishment but also explicit reference to coinage. Such a document, it bears repeating, would be unimaginable in a Spartan context.

Realities of Spartan Financing

That said, the realities of resources on both sides were more complex. The Peloponnesians had a fleet that, even in one of the early theaters of the war (principally, the Corinthian Gulf), was effective enough to cause the Athenian side some real difficulties. The financing of the fleet, however, had to come largely from allied Peloponnesian cities. Traditionally, agrarian, land-based Sparta did not mint coins and indeed was ideologically opposed to the use of coined money (though this glosses over the reality of elite Spartans' possession of money; one example among many: a whopping 10,000 drachma fine, with which King Agis in 418 was threatened for his failure to engage the enemy at Nemea [Thuc. 5.63.2]). But, as we saw in the previous chapter, some of their allies (Corinth and its colonies) were capable of producing a sizable war chest when need arose. Beginning in 431, such a need occurred on a large scale.

The Spartan coalition could look to the mint of Corinth for coinage to support its own fleet. But, oriented to Corinthian commerce and interests in the west, Corinthian staters on a 8.6 g standard, did not circulate in the Peloponnese, which was long accustomed to using money on the heavier 12.2 g stater standard of Aegina. Over much of the fifth century, two major allies of Sparta did mint staters and fractions on the Aeginetan standard: Thebes in Boeotia and, in the northwest Peloponnese, the city of Elis, which administered the Festival of Zeus at Olympia (Fig. 5.1), but both cities minted chiefly for local, regional use.

The several other Peloponnesian cities that minted in the fifth century struck only in small to minuscule denominations of Aeginetan weight – usually half-drachmas down to the quarter of an obol (0.25 g) – in order

a.   b.

Figure 5.1 Silver staters of Elis and Thebes (mid-fifth century BC). Aeginetan standard. (a) Stater of **Elis** depicting an eagle seizing a hare; on the reverse a winged thunderbolt and the letters F-A (= WA for *Wa[lion]*, the local spelling for "[*of the*] *Elians*"). The eagle and thunderbolt are attributes of Zeus. 12.11 g. *ANS*. (b) Stater of **Thebes**, with the types of a Boeotian shield and a wine amphora, a symbol of Dionysos. The letters Θ-E on the reverse are the initial letters of the city name. 11.93 g. *ANS*.

locally to supplement the silver staters of Aegina, which circulated so ubiquitously in southern Greece that they came to be regarded as a general Peloponnesian coinage. Nevertheless, owing to Athens' subjugation of Aegina in 457, the availability of Aeginetan staters was in decline. The tortoise staters struck by Aegina after 457, discussed in the preceding chapter, did nothing to increase the supply of this money since every new stater minted merely replaced an older one on which it was overstruck (pp. 76–7). Moreover, if Athens' expulsion of the Aeginetans from their island in 431 did not stop the coining of tortoises altogether, any continuation of the coinage at the Aeginetan exile polis of Thyrea in the northeast Peloponnesos would have been ended seven years later by the Athenian sack of that city and capture of its survivors (Thuc. 4.57.1–3).

Just to the west of Corinth, however, was its neighbor Sikyon, relatively unsung at this time in the literary evidence, but, to judge from the numismatic record, a powerhouse in the Peloponnesians' war effort. Along with the onset of war and the Peloponnesians' need for a reliable, new source of coin, the city undertook production of a copious series of exquisitely designed, Aeginetan-weight staters (Fig. 5.2). As Sikyon had minted previously only in sporadic, fractional denominations, the launching of this stater coinage represented a major initiative. Its duration, from the late 430s to the early years of the fourth century, roughly paralleled that of the Peloponnesian War. Because its scale (more than 128 obverse dies over some thirty-odd years) was far more substantial than that of ordinary civic coinages, there is reason to think that it may have been supported by other

Figure 5.2 Silver stater of **Sikyon** (last third of the fifth century BC). Aeginetan standard. The dove on the obverse is the dove of Aphrodite, a major deity of the city. On the reverse is the mythological beast known as the Chimaera and the letters ΣΕ, for Si(kyonians) in an early spelling. 12.04 g. *ANS.*

cities of the Peloponnesian alliance and was principally intended to help finance the war (Warren 2000; 2009).

To this extent, numismatic evidence helps us understand how it was that the Spartans were able to mobilize a fleet and operate at sea during the early years of the Peloponnesian War just as it illuminates the Corcyrean-Corinthian conflict preceding the war.

The Settlement after the Revolt of Mytilene in 428–427 BC

In the early years of the war the Athenians had to contend with annual Spartan invasions, major campaigns in the northwest, and a devastating plague that killed thousands upon thousands, while still maintaining the costly siege of Poteidaia (which they brought to an end in 429). Soon they were faced with further revolts that broke out on the island of Lesbos and in the Chalkidike. These revolts engendered monetary transformations in two critical regions of the *arche*. For this reason we now turn to these events. It should be noted that these transformations go unmentioned in our written sources, although they, and in particular, Thucydides, give prominence to the political significance of these revolts and their effects.

Mytilene, the rich and most powerful city of Lesbos, revolted in 428, having intended to for some time and hoping for Sparta's support. The city had been one of Athens' most valuable allies, providing ships and men instead of paying tribute. In addition to its large territory on Lesbos, Mytilene possessed seven cities on the adjacent mainland along the western extension of the Troad known as the Akte.

The revolt failed when an Athenian force arrived at the island and the promised Spartan assistance failed to materialize in time. The Mytilenians were compelled to surrender, tear down their walls, and give up their ships. More than a thousand Mytilenians were put to death, and the seven

Aktaian cities were freed from Mytilenian control and made tributary allies of Athens. As we learn further from Thucydides (3.50), instead of making Mytilene and two lesser cities on Lesbos that participated in the rebellion pay tribute, Athens confiscated their land and divided it into 3,000 allotments, 300 of which were designated sacred property, and the rest granted to Athenian cleruchs who were sent out from Athens and were to rent out the land to Lesbians to work for an annual fee of 200 drachmas per allotment. With this settlement, the amount of money that was to be paid to the gods and the cleruchs in rents would come to a total of 100 talents each year, of which ten, the gods' tithe, were to be paid into Athens' sacred treasury.

Following upon this drastic restructuring of their territory, the Mytilenians, who had been minting their distinguished coinage of electrum *hektai* (Fig. 3.4) and an internal, small-denomination coinage of billon, a silver-copper alloy of less than 50 percent silver (Ellis-Evans 2018, 189–90, 224–7) (Fig. 5.3a), introduced their first-ever coinage of pure silver, which consisted of drachmas weighing about 4 g (Fig. 5.3b) and corresponding hemidrachms, obols, and hemiobols. What is fascinating is that, when

a.

b.

Figure 5.3 Coins of **Mytilene**. (**a**) Fractional coin of billon (probably 430s BC). Obverse head of the nymph Mytilene and reverse head of a lion with the initials M-Y. 1.95 g. *Gorny (2013)*. (**b**) Silver drachma (427–*c*. 404 BC). Attic standard. Obverse and reverse heads of Apollo and the nymph Mytilene respectively. The ethnic reads from the upper left [M]ΥΤΙ-ΛΗ-ΝΑΟ-Ν ("Of the Mytilenians"). 3.94 g. *Paris*. Hemidrachms, obols, and hemiobols were struck along with the drachma, as they were also for most of the coinages illustrated in Figs. 5.4 and 5.5.

allowance is made for the common Greek practice of minting local small denominations slightly below standard, it is apparent that these new coins were adjusted to the weight values and denominational structure of Athenian coinage.

In a study involving a great many fractional coins that have become known only in the past two decades, Aneurin Ellis-Evans and Jonathan Kagan demonstrate that this Mytilenian coinage was only the first of fifteen new or refashioned silver coinages of reduced Attic weight in the region, typically in small denominational units from the drachma to the half-obol (Ellis-Evans 2018, 190–196; Ellis-Evans and Kagan, in preparation; Erol-Özdizbay 2018, 68, 73, 78). Three of these coinages were signed and issued by the newly autonymous Aktaian cities of Pordoselene, Antandros, and Larisa (Fig. 5.4), which, as former dependencies of Mytilene, had been using the electrum and billon currency of that city, never having minted before on their own. These three new coinages' common format, fine style, and conspicuous lettering are shared with the new coinage at Mytilene, showing that all four coinages were produced in a coordinated program and at a single mint, which would have been the long-established mint at Mytilene. The remaining Attic-weight coinages come from nearby cities in the Troad and Aeolis (Fig. 5.5). Several of these, too, were first-time

a.

b.

c.

Figure 5.4 Silver Attic-weight coins of the newly autonomous Aktaian cities of the Troad (427–*c.* 404 BC). (a) Drachma of **Pordoselene** depicting the head of Apollo and, on the reverse, his lyre, around which runs the abbreviated ethnic ΠΟΡΔ-ΟΣΙΛ. 4.03 g. *Lanz (2009).* (b) Drachma of **Antandros** depicting the head of Artemis and a goat; inscribed ANTA-N. 3.84 g. *Gorny (2008).* (c) Hemidrachm of **Larisa**, with the types of a nymph head and amphora; inscribed ΛΑΡΙΣΑΙ. 2.03 g. *CNG (2014).*

Figure 5.5 Silver Attic-weight hemidrachms of three other cities of the Troad (c. 427–404 BC). (**a**) Hemidrachm of **Lamponeia**, with a bearded male head and, on the reverse, the head of a bull; inscribed ΛΑΜ. 1.82 g. *ANS.* (**b**) Hemidrachm of **Gargara**, with a young male head and, on the reverse, a galloping horse; inscribed ΓΑΡ. 2.27 g. *Oxford.* (**c**) Hemidrachm of **Neandreia**, with laureate head of Apollo and on the reverse, an altar before a laurel tree; inscribed N-E (below) A-N. 1.95 g. *Lanz (2004).*

minters: Neandreia, Gergis, and perhaps Dardanos in the Troad; Myrina, Pitane, and Pergamon (obols only) in Aeolis. The rest (all in the Troad: Assos, Gargara, Lamponeia, Kebren, and Skepsis) had minted previously in small denominations, mostly obols.

Athens' defeat of Mytilene in 427, with the consequent loss of its land and its mainland possessions, must have provided the impetus for the creation of the new, atticizing local currency at Mytilene and the Aktaian cities, which in turn motivated its spread to other cities in the area that recognized the benefit of adopting it themselves. Since two of the cities, Gergis and Pergamon, are not known to have been members of the Athenian *arche*, we appear not to be dealing here with an Athenian mandate. In fact, it would probably be mistaken to think that the Athenians imposed this small-unit silver coinage even at Mytilene and the Aktaian cities, for Athens would have gained nothing by doing so. What Athens did impose on Lesbos, as mentioned earlier, were the hundred talents of annual rents that were to be paid to resident and absentee Athenian landowners and into the sacred treasury of the gods at Athens, principally Athena, while on the freed Aktaian cities, Athens imposed annual payments of tribute. These large obligations were denominated in Athenian money and in all probability were expected to be paid in Athenian silver tetradrachms or their local equivalents in electrum, Mytilenian *hektai* (Fig. 3.4), which happened to be valued at four Athenian drachmas each (Melville Jones 1998, 263n). Although it is reasonable to assume that Mytilene's minting in electrum was halted with the suppression of the revolt in 427, there is at present no reliable evidence when it resumed (O&R, p. 577). The resumption of the coinage has been thought to date after 404 BC, or at 412, but an even earlier dating cannot be excluded. A great quantity of the *hektai* remained in circulation nevertheless and would have continued in use as before.

Smaller denomination currency for everyday internal transactions was, however, an entirely different matter, and, as we see from the local ethnics and types of the new small-denomination coins, their provision was undertaken by the cities. Needing to replace its idiosyncratic and excessively overvalued billon currency by divisions that were compatible with the higher value coins required for payments to Athenians and Athens, Mytilene, followed by the other cities, turned to striking a conventional small-unit silver coinage structured on the Athenian model. Altogether, the minting of these Attic-weight drachmas and fractions by Mytilene, by the mainland cities detached from its control, and then by nearby cities in an expanding radius, is the most compelling evidence we have for the growth of Athenian monetary influence in a single region of the *arche*.

Revolts in the Chalkidike, 432–421

As we saw in the previous chapter, the Athenians' successful takeover of Amphipolis in 437/436 capped their attempts to gain control over the lower Strymon and its access to the resources of the interior that began with the takeover of Eïon in 476. But securing Amphipolis may well have been the tipping point of an increasingly volatile geopolitical, economic balance in the intense competition for control of these resources.

Relations between Athens and the Macedonian King Perdikkas II were precarious. Initially an ally and supplier of timber to the Athenians, Perdikkas turned against them and sought to detach Athens' subjects in the Chalkidike, not only because of the Athenians' control of Amphipolis but also because by the mid- to late 430s they had allied themselves with Perdikkas' brother, Philip. When the Athenians became embroiled in their conflict with Corinth and ordered its colony Poteidaia to break all ties with Corinth (p. 87), Perdikkas saw an opportunity to take advantage by encouraging Poteidaia and a number of lesser Chalkidian poleis in the immediate region to revolt. This they did in 432 with the Poteidaians even entering into the confederacy (*koinon*) of the Chalkidians. With Perdikkas' support, the Chalkidians on the coast actually destroyed their cities and moved inland to Olynthos, making it a populous stronghold of the confederacy, and assisted the Poteidaians – a mere six miles away – in resisting the Athenian siege. Perdikkas' ability to capitalize on the unrest in the area at this time and into the 420s had profound consequences: besides encouraging the cities to revolt, his tactics led to a shift in the political and economic orientation of much of the entire peninsula toward independence from Athens and closer engagement with Macedon, a shift that that is epitomized in the coinage.

Prior to the later 430s, Akanthos, Mende, and those few other cities that were still coining, did so on the Euboean weight standard with a stater of *c.* 17 g and *hektai* of 2.8 g (pp. 52–5). Within a little more than a decade, however, minting on this traditional standard of the peninsula had been largely replaced by the coining of lighter, 2.3–2.4 g *hektai* of a reduced, Milesian-weight standard (stater of *c.* 14 g), the standard used by Perdikkas and earlier in some of the coinage of his father, Alexander I (Psoma 2015a, 173–4). During his reign Perdikkas coined in these light *hektai* exclusively (Fig. 5.6). As one might expect from Perdikkas' active support of insurrection in the Chalkidike, hoards attest that his *hektai* circulated there in quantity.

Let us move to Olynthos. Coinciding with the revolts of the minor Chalkidian cities and the relocation of their populations to Olynthos appear the only coins that were ever minted with the name of the Olynthians: Milesian-weight *hektai* with the types of a horse and an upright flying eagle (Fig. 5.7a,b), types that are continued from the earlier Euboean-weight *hektai* that were minted in the name of the Chalkidians (Fig. 3.11a) when the Euboean weight standard was still the dominant monetary standard of the region. In sharp contrast, when the Chalkidians at Olynthos minted these *hektai* inscribed OΛYN, they employed the lighter, Milesian weight of Perdikkas' *hektai* – as well as the odd technique of royal Macedonian minting that, in contrast to routine Greek practice (see Fig. 1.4), employed a larger number of obverse than reverse dies. These Macedonian features

Figure 5.6 Silver *hekte* of King **Perdikkas II** of Macedon (struck late 430s–420s BC). Milesian standard. The types – a horseman wearing a hat with a brim and holding two spears, and the forepart of a lion – were continued from the *hektai* of Perdikkas' father, Alexander I. Like other coins of Perdikkas, this one is uninscribed. 2.41 g. *ANS.*

a.   b.

Figure 5.7 Silver *hektai* of the confederated **Chalkidians** at Olynthos (*c.* 432–early 420s BC). Milesian standard. Only the obverse types differ: the horse on (**a**) is jumping; the horse on (**b**) stands, tethered to a column. Both reverses depict an upright, flying eagle holding a snake and have letters in the corners of the incuse square that give the abbreviated ethnic, O-Λ-Y-N. (**a**) 2.13 g. *ANS.* (**b**) 2.42 g. *ANS.*

make a strong implicit case that the Olynthian coins commenced around 432, when Perdikkas became actively involved in Chalkidian affairs and promoted the Chalkidian revolt centered on a strong and enlarged base at Olynthos (Psoma 2001, 177–8).

In 424 Perdikkas, together with the confederated Chalkidians at Olynthos, urged the Spartan commander Brasidas to invade the Chalkidike with Perdikkas himself promising to pay half of the cost of the Spartan force (Thuc. 4.83.5–6) – which came to number some seven hundred helot hoplites sent by Sparta and a thousand Peloponnesian mercenaries recruited by Brasidas himself. To the extent that Perdikkas was to pay for half of Brasidas' force in his own coinage, it would have to have been with bags of his 2.4 g *hektai* (Fig. 5.6). There is good reason to think that the Chalkidians initiated a new series of *hektai* with the obverse head of Apollo at this time and that because its first phase was exceptional in size, employing seventeen obverse and thirteen reverse dies, its purpose was to provide money for the Peloponnesian army as well (Kagan 2014, 13–14; Psoma 2001, 170–9, 186). Although minted at Olynthos, the coinage is now again signed by the confederated Chalkidians (Fig. 5.8).

Another, and potentially greater source of coin in the Chalkidike, was the polis of Akanthos, long the most productive minter of silver coins in the region and Brasidas' first destination upon his arrival in the Chalkidike – whether because of its strategic importance or specifically because of its mint. Thucydides says that despite the Akanthians' initial reluctance to renounce their allegiance to Athens, Brasidas managed to win them over – after threatening to destroy their grape harvest. Along with their revolt from Athens and realignment with Brasidas in 424, the Akanthians stopped striking Euboean-weight staters and *hektai* (Fig. 3.9) and, changing standard,

Figure 5.8 Silver *hekte* of the confederated **Chalkidians** at Olynthos (424 into the fourth century BC). Milesian Standard. The head of Apollo on the obverse is paired with a reverse type of his lyre around which is inscribed ΧΑΛ-ΚΙΔ-Ε-ΩΝ ("Of the Chalcidians"). 2.23 g. ANS.

a.   b.

Figure 5.9 Silver Milesian-weight coins of **Akanthos** (post 424 BC). (a) Stater, displaying a lion mauling a bull, and on the reverse the ethnic ΑΚΑ-Ν-ΘΙΟ-Ν around a four-part square. 14.24 g. ANS. (b) *Hekte*, with the forepart of a bull with turned head on the obverse. 2.25 g. ANS.

began to coin in lighter Milesian-weight staters and, on a truly colossal scale, *hektai* (Fig. 5.9; Kagan 2014, 14). Now the most prolific coinage in the Chalkidike, there can be little doubt of the importance of this lighter Akanthian coinage for Brasidas and his Peloponnesian army.

Indeed, Brasidas' needs for funding were considerable. After Akanthos, the Spartan general captured Amphipolis and was successful in supporting numerous revolts throughout the peninsula. When in the summer of 422 he had to defend Amphipolis against the large force sent out from Athens under the command of Kleon, Brasidas was assembling an army of at least 5,000 Greek and Thracian fighters (Thuc. 5.6.4–5). In battle, the Athenians were defeated, but Brasidas was killed, as was Kleon a major advocate of war. And because both sides had experienced significant reversals – Sparta, the ignominious and unprecedented surrender of many hoplites at Sphakteria in Messenia in 425, and Athens, the loss of so many cities in the north – Sparta and Athens turned toward making peace.

Figure 5.10 Silver Milesian-weight *hekte* of **Terone** (after 424 BC).T-E on either side of a wine pitcher identifies the issuing city as Terone (compare Fig. 3.8*a*). 2.14 g. *ANS.*

Among the major cities of the Chalkidike that revolted in 423 but were later recaptured by the Athenians within a year or two, Mende, which had always minted on the Euboean-weight standard, continued to do so, although only in *hektai* (Fig. 3.10c) and smaller denominations (Kagan 2014, 17–8). Every other coining city in the Chalkidike had gone over to minting on the lighter standard of Perdikkas and the Chalkidians. Even the city of Terone, which had not coined for decades (Fig. 3.8a), and was, like Mende, still allied with Athens at the time of the Peace, initiated a substantial coinage of *hektai* (Fig. 5.10) on the lighter 2.4 g standard, either because it may have later revoked its allegiance to Athens (Kagan 2014, 16n) or because by the later 420s, the lighter standard had become the nearly exclusive silver currency standard of the region.

In a critical clause of the Peace of Nikias (as it is conventionally known), concluded in the spring of 421, Amphipolis was to be returned to Athens, and with its return, the Athenians would have expected to regain their control of the precious metal and timber that possession of the colony gave them. But this did not happen, and never would, despite concerted efforts to regain the city over the next many decades. Some might term it an obsession – in the mid-fourth century the Athenians were still fixated on gaining this former possession – which only reinforces what the Strymon River valley, and access to silver mines and timber, meant to them.

What the empire meant to Athens as shown by the Peace is another important question. Salient is that by the terms of the Peace the Athenians kept their empire. However, some tucked-in terms that applied to six cities in the north that had been taken by Brasidas (Thuc. 5.18.5) are harbingers of a sea change in thinking about the relationship between Athens and the cities under its control. Those cities, including Akanthos and Olynthos, were to pay tribute as "in the time of Aristeides", that is, at the level assessed in 478, but they could remain autonomous or join the Athenian alliance. The concession of independence must have come from the cities and have been a bargaining chip, but in name only, because if they were compelled to pay tribute they certainly did not have independence. From the cities' perspectives the difference between being subjects of Athens paying tribute and "independent" paying tribute will perhaps have varied. But of course the Athenians' chief concern was revenue; the simplest way of formulating that goal was through *phoros*. That *phoros* was unsatisfactory as a means of revenue, however, became clear shortly into the Peace. We turn to that next.

6

The Peace of Nikias and the Rethinking of Monetary Policy, 421–413 BC

The peace treaty and alliance concluded by Athens and Sparta in 421 were intended to last fifty years. They lasted eight. Even so, Thucydides famously rejected the notion that the Peace of Nikias was a real peace (5.26), punctuated as it was by one of the largest land battles of the entire war (at Mantinea in 418), ineffectual alliances, and renewals of hostilities. He therefore reconstructed the war as one long, twenty-seven-year conflict, an historiographical decision that turned out to have an immense influence. But if we set that aside for a moment and appreciate the perspective most Athenians and other Greeks would have had, a different picture emerges. As with the earlier "Thirty Years Peace" of 446 (which lasted fifteen years), Athens was left with its empire essentially intact, and, freed from the constraints of war with Sparta, could turn to unfinished business and the making of large-scale plans.

The unfinished business included the subjugation of Melos, a large Cycladic island originally colonized by Sparta, and one that successfully resisted an attempt by Athens in 427 to add it to its dominion. At the southern perimeter of the *arche* in the Aegean, and rich in resources such as obsidian, Melos was an obvious target for conquest; leaving the island alone to enjoy its independence, while all other islands in the region were subject to Athens, only reflected Athens' – as Thucydides represents it – weakness (5.95). So, in 416, taking advantage of the Peace and recovered finances, the Athenians made a second attempt. When reading Thucydides' famous Melian Dialogue (5.85–112), one might get the impression that the island was an easy target – one island against the mighty power of Athens. Not so. The Athenians crushed Melos only after a lengthy siege and assisted by treachery within the city. In the aftermath of the siege and surrender, all the men, women, and children that were rounded up were either slaughtered, in the case of the men, or enslaved, as was the fate of the women and children. The island became an Athenian possession with 500 settlers (Thuc. 5.114–16), as we have mentioned earlier.

Unlike the Cycladic islands that were within the Athenian *arche*, and did not mint beyond the 450s, Melos had minted continuously into the last

a.   b.

Figure 6.1 Two of over eighty varied silver staters of **Melos**, recovered in 1907 in a hoard buried on the island in 416 BC (*IGCH* 27; Kraay 1964; Sheedy 2006: 68–71). Milesian standard. Their obverse type of an apple (*mēlon* in Greek) is a punning device on the name of the city. There were at least twenty-four different reverse types of this coinage, all inscribed with the ethnic ΜΑΛΙΟΝ ("Of the Melians" in the Doric dialect), sometimes abbreviated. (**a**) Reverse type of three dolphins swimming around a central boss. 13.66 g. *ANS.* (**b**) Reverse type of a square divided into triangles. 13.94 g. *ANS.*

quarter of the century, reflecting its independence, until the islanders were conquered by Athens. The last phases of this coinage are especially well known from a hoard of about a hundred staters that were buried in a pot on the island at the time of the Athenian attack (*IGCH* 27). Figure 6.1 illustrates two staters from the hoard.

Next, more unfinished business and the large-scale plans. Also in 427, Athens had sent an expeditionary force to Sicily, in response to a request of its ally Leontini, threatened by its powerful neighbor, Syracuse. According to Thucydides, Athens was motivated by further objectives, first, to explore the feasibility of conquering the island, and, second, to halt the commerce in grain to the Peloponnesos. This intervention too had failed in its objectives. The Peace, however, allowed the Athenians to revive their interest in Sicily, this time occasioned not only by the Leontinians but also by a request for aid from another ally, Egesta, a non-Greek, but hellenized city in northwestern Sicily (Fig. 6.2), at war with its formidable neighbor to the south, Selinos, an ally of the Syracusans. Following the takeover of Melos, the Athenians launched a major expedition to Sicily ostensibly to help the Egestaians but with a larger target in mind, namely, Syracuse, the most powerful and richest city in the Greek West, its wealth reflected in its impressive silver coinage (Figs. 6.3 and 7.1). Conquering Syracuse was for the Athenians the key to gaining control of Sicily. To confirm their intentions, one need only look at the locations of their military activity on the island: they concentrated on the east coast at and around Syracuse. Egesta and Selinos, however, were in the west.

Figure 6.2 Silver didrachm of **Egesta**, Sicily (420s BC), with the head of the nymph Egesta and the reverse type of a hound. Uninscribed. Attic standard. 8.45 g. *ANS*. The head of the nymph is unskillfully copied from the Arethusa head of the Syracusan tetradrachm, Fig. 6.3. The minting of a silver coinage based on Greek models was one of several practices that the indigenous Sicilians of Egesta adopted in emulation of Hellenic polis culture.

Figure 6.3 Silver tetradrachm of **Syracuse** (420s BC), depicting a four-horse racing chariot with a winged Victory flying above to crown the victorious charioteer; and, on the reverse, the head of Arethusa, the nymph of the spring in the center of the city, around which are swimming four dolphins; inscribed counterclockwise ΣΥΡΑ-ΚΟ-ΣΙΟΝ ("Of the Syracusians"). Attic standard. 17.01 g. *ANS*.

The Egestaians, who had promised to finance an Athenian expedition in toto, were duplicitous, as it turned out. While they showed up initially at Athens with sixty talents of silver bullion – an amount to fund sixty ships for one month – when the Athenians were about to cross over from Italy to Sicily, a mere thirty talents was all that the Egestaians could produce, a very far cry from the cash needed to pay the fleet sent by Athens and its allies for an extended campaign.

The absence of expected funding came as a shock to the Athenian generals, except for Nikias, forcing them to raise sufficient funds from other sources if they were to carry on the expedition at all (Thuc. 6.46–7). Thucydides, earlier, refers to the "vast amount of money" taken out of Athens; but his focus is mostly on private expenditures on the splendid appearance of the ships and their fittings ("it was the most expensive and prettiest," and its renown among other Greeks was based on "its daring and the magnificence of its appearance" [6.31.6]).

Documentary evidence of what the Athenians took with them to Sicily is fragmentary, and a matter of scholarly dispute over its value, given that it depends on restorations – always fertile territory for controversy. The evidence comes in the form of a fragmentary decree (O&R 171) thought to pertain to the preparations for the expedition, which include a reference to a "thousand," restored as "three thousand talents" earmarked for the expedition; but it is not certain whether the figure refers to money or something else, and it is doubtful that in 415 the Athenians, expecting funding from Egesta, would have allocated such a large amount for the campaign before discovering the Egestaians' insolvency (Kallet 2001, 183–205). Another inscription, recording four payments out of Athena's treasury from the years 418–414 for generals in Sicily, is again fragmentary but in any case cannot be reconciled with presumed massive expenditures on the expedition. A further fragmentary document lists contributions by Sicilian cities, such as Naxos and Katana, but whether they relate to the campaign in 427, mentioned earlier, or that of 415, is unclear. In short, while we should probably assume substantial payments coming out of Athena's treasury in addition to the 300 and 150 talent supplements mentioned by Thucydides (p. 24), the evidence leaves many questions unanswered.

Taxes and Revenue: Rethinking the *Arche*

During the Peace the Athenians decided upon a radical reorientation of the *arche's* revenue structure. Thucydides provides the sole evidence for the innovation, which replaced tribute with an empire-wide maritime tax of 5 percent (*eikoste*). The context in which he places it, however, is renewed war in 413 (7.28. 3–4):

> Now, seventeen years after that first invasion, and by now completely exhausted by the war, they went to Sicily and took on a new war just as onerous as their longstanding conflict with the Peloponnese. All this, combined now with the huge damage being inflicted by [the fort at] Dekeleia, and other costs hitting hard, had crippled them financially. It was around this time that they imposed on their subject allies, in place of tribute, a five-percent tax on seaborne goods, on the grounds that this would bring them greater income. Their expenses had not

remained at the earlier level, but had grown considerably as the war had grown, and their revenues were failing. (Trans. Hammond, adapted)

Thucydides' phrasing, a 5 percent tax on, literally, "the things by sea," refers to a tax on cargo, a tax known, from universal practice in antiquity, to have been levied on both imports and exports (Fawcett 2016, 160–1; Gabrielsen 2013, 339–41; Purcell 2005, 210, 223–5). While there is no reason to doubt Thucydides' relative chronology about the implementation ("around this time," writing of events in winter 413), we need to question the context of the decision-making that led to the substitution of the tax for tribute: the historian represents the *eikoste* as an emergency wartime solution to declining revenue, implying that the decision was made on the spot in the midst of formally renewed war.

In fact, wartime was the last context in which citizens in the Assembly would have thought a maritime tax would bring in more revenue than any other form of income. Maritime trade flourished in peacetime. (Aristophanes' play, *Merchant Ships*, mentioned earlier, was categorized by an ancient commentator as one of his "peace plays.") At times of conflict, cargo ships were sought-after targets – indeed, one of the opening violent acts of the Peloponnesian War was the Spartans' slaughter of merchants, from neutral as well as enemy states, circumnavigating the Peloponnese (Thuc. 2.67.4). With the Peace, however, Athenians would have had reason to think about the profits of commerce, with taxation at the center. From this vantage point we need to consider two other critical issues: the rationale for the change, and the length of time that it would have taken from planning to implementation of the tax.

First, the rationale. Underlying the tax was a wholesale rethinking about the extraction of resources from the *arche* and the relationship between that rethinking and the Athenians' conceptualizing of their empire as an economic and commercial entity. The question is why. To answer this question we need to look back. During the war, Athens' expenditures, unsurprisingly, increased dramatically. Perhaps also unsurprising was that its subjects would take the opportunity of war to renege on their tributary obligations. Financial problems emerged as early as 428, when the richest Athenians had to pay a direct poll tax – abhorrent for Greeks – which yielded 200 talents (Thuc. 3.19).

The epigraphic record, in particular, speaks volumes. Around 426 the Athenians passed a decree on the motion of Kleonymos ordering an empire-wide improvement in tribute collection through the appointment of local tribute collectors in the cities who, presumably, were personally responsible for ensuring that the full amounts were paid (O&R 152, *AIO*; see Fig. 1.2). In the following year, 425, they approved an extraordinary reassessment of tribute in which they increased the amounts many cities were to pay, at least twice or threefold what they had paid previously. Another huge marble stele (as imposing as the Lapis Primus) was set up on the Acropolis to publicize the decision in the boldest, one might say, intimidating way (O&R 153, *AIO*); Athens meant business. But their subjects, it appears, were not cowed by the projection of power in the decree. Hardly a stone, even the tiniest inscribed fragment, has been found to support Athens' success in collecting anything approaching the new assessment imposed on these cities (which, incidentally, contained a number that were never known to have paid, or even to have been in the *arche*, such as Melos). Yet the editors of *The Athenian Tribute Lists* tenaciously resisted the possibility that the goals of the assessment were not met. Such a possibility, however, deserves to be taken seriously (Kallet 2004, 492–5): if the Athenians had had difficulties reaching targets of tribute, increasing those targets was certainly not a realistic remedy. A decree likely following the 425 reassessment speaks directly to the continuation of the crisis, as evidenced partly by the increased involvement of the Council (or *Boule*) of 500, the body most closely involved in the city's domestic and imperial finances. On a proposal by Kleinias, it outlines a complex procedure of identification seals to forestall evidently widespread corruption and fraud at various points in the conveying of a city's tribute to Athens (O&R 154, *AIO*). The unreliability and difficulty of the tributary system comprises the essential background for understanding the Athenians' decision to eliminate this fiscal – and politically charged – institution.

It is important to appreciate that it would not have been an easy sell to convince a majority of Athenians to dismantle tribute, an institution that in a fundamental respect had defined the empire and the Athenians' power over their subjects since 478 – a heady mix for the average Athenian. Moreover, because a considerable amount of planning and advance organizing were required for such a complex and bold initiative, the time between conception and implementation ought to have spanned at least a year or more, meaning that the initiative had originated and been developed before Sicily and Dekeleia, during a time of peace with Sparta.

That said, all would have been familiar with the profitability of maritime taxes, especially the ubiquitous 2 percent customs duties on imports and exports, the most lucrative source of income by far for all cities with active harbors. For their part, the Athenians had had experience exploiting the resources of the *arche* through their control over key *emporia* in the north and the Hellespontine traffic, which in effect created a closed sea and therefore yielded profit from taxes levied on ships that passed through the narrow strait from the Black Sea (via the Bosphoros and Propontis) to the Aegean. The Athenians, in short, had long made it their business to control maritime commerce within their realm.

In the context of a well-established tributary empire, the new tax policy was an innovation, even a revolutionary one, just as the Athenians' creation of a tributary empire was in its Greek context. Politically both were radical, but economically, at this time, the maritime tax made common sense. From the cities' standpoint, the persons affected may have been different from those required to produce tribute: we lack firm evidence of who was responsible for paying tribute, but we know that this tax would have fallen upon merchants, including non-citizens, more than the cities; at the same time, the Athenians may have supposed that this measure would have constituted less of a sting than tribute, with all of its symbolic as well as practical implications (Kallet 2001, 211–12, 217). But the essential point is that trade meant profit. All cities with ports exacted maritime taxes in their own territory; for the Athenians, their "own territory" now comprised the entire *arche*.

We can only guess at the details of how the *eikoste* was to be organized. In Greek cities the collecting of cargo taxes was normally privatized, farmed out to individuals or a syndicate that bid to operate the franchise for the state (best documented from Athens in Andokides, *On the Mysteries*, 133–4, with the reference to the *pentekoste*, the 2 percent tax). Obliged to pay to the state the amount they proposed in their bid, they were able to keep any surplus as profit. For the tax farmers the system was not without risk since they owed the state the contractual amount whether or not they were able to collect it in taxes; consequently, they had to produce evidence of substantial financial backing as part of the bidding process and make a down payment. While the procedure was straightforward enough to be routinely administered by single cities, the challenge faced by the Athenians in collecting the *eikoste* from the scores of port cities in their *arche* was centrally managing all of the local collecting in a way that ensured that the proceeds would be fairly, fully, and regularly obtained and passed on to Athens.

The Athenian planners would have had access to whatever past tax records and bidding contracts the cities within their sphere of power kept and so would have been able to estimate future income from the *eikoste*. They also would have drawn on the decades of their own experience on taxing maritime commerce abroad. From the 470s Athens had profited from the taxes it imposed at *emporia*, first at Eïon at the mouth of the Strymon and then along the string of *emporia* on the Thracian littoral seized from Thasos. At the Hellespont, the "Guards of the Hellespont" (*Hellespontophylakes*) had operated a customs house no later than the beginning of the Peloponnesian War (attested in the Methone decree, O&R 150; *AIO*). They exacted a cargo and transit tax on every ship that passed through that narrow strait.

Even so, the establishment of the *eikoste* called for a wide range of new decisions. Would the new tax be over and above existing taxes in the cities that had harbors? There would need to be new officials, like the *eikostologos* on Aegina who appears in Aristophanes' *Frogs* (line 363)– Aegina at that time was inhabited by Athenians, but we cannot tell from this reference whether the official was a local Athenian or from Athens. Would the tax farmers be selected in a bidding system? What would their qualifications be? Would they be locals in the cities? Should Athenians have a role? Directives, too, presumably had to be drawn up about the keeping of tax records, so that they could be sent to Athens for audit (the Athenians were meticulous about transparency and accountability especially when it came to money and finances). Whatever was decided, the procedures had to be standardized across the *arche*, along with the instruments of taxation: the weights and measures necessary for assessing the values of cargoes and the currency in which the assessments were expressed and paid. However suitable local systems of measurement and currency might be for local taxation, for the kind of global taxation embodied by the Athenian *eikoste*, efficiency and transparency in assessment, payment, and auditing demanded that the standards of measurement and currency be global as well.

Standardization: The Coinage, Weights, and Measures Decree

The *eikoste* provides a compelling rationale for legislation that ensured that standardization was in place prior to the implementation of the *arche*-wide customs taxation. It can hardly be mere coincidence that, as we learn from

Aristophanes' *Birds*, another Athenian enactment seemingly from around this same time deals with this very issue. The comedy concerns the founding of a new settlement in the sky. Along comes a decree-seller – what could a new city be without decrees! – and peddles one in particular (lines 1037–40):

DECREE-SELLER: *I am a seller of decrees, and I have come here to sell you new laws.*

PISTHETAIROS: *Such as?*

DECREE-SELLER: *The people of Cloudcuckooland are to use the same weights, measures, and decrees (psephísmata) as the Olophyxians.*

Aristophanes' audience would have easily recognized this allusion to an actual decree, and that, in his play on words the poet substituted "decrees" (*psephismata*) for "coins" (*nomismata*). This reference, the sole ancient mention of the decree, implies that it was passed (or was at least prominent in public discussion) shortly before the play was performed in March 414. (Well before any stone fragments of the Coinage, Weights, and Measures Decree had been discovered, the formidable German scholar Wilamowitz von Moellendorf posited the existence of a decree concerning weights, measures, and *coins* on the basis of this comic reference alone.)

No complete copy of a single decree survives. And missing from all of the surviving fragments are the opening sentences that would have given the dating and administrative formulas. We infer from the oath of the Boule in some fragments (e.g., Aphytis and Smyrna) that the subject of the documents was an order to their subject allies to use the coins, weights, and measures of Athens. Other sentences are concerned with details about the transmission of the decree and some provisions related to publicizing and implementing, including the setting up of the inscriptions in the local cities, and the procedure for bringing coins to Athens for reminting. Of the portions that have been found, comparisons are intriguing indeed: there is enough overlap to see identical clauses in a number of instances, or enough parts of one fragment to allow confident restorations in another. There are also some minor deviations (word order and the like) without at all affecting meaning. But one size, evidently, does not fit all, because there are a few significant discrepancies.

Perhaps the most significant of these is the differing length of the decree because it suggests that not all cities were given identical instructions. Given the happenstance nature of epigraphic finds, it is pure luck that the end of one decree has been found (the most recently discovered of two fragments from Aphytis), which contains an oath. But in another inscribed fragment of the decree, the one found near Smyrna, the similar oath appears, but it is not the end of the document: the oath is followed by several more lines of text. We shall consider implications of these and other differences later. Let us first examine what has led scholars to assume a single, "composite" decree issued to all members of the *arche*, attested by the existence of fragments unearthed in disparate regions of the *arche* (see Map 6.1).

Map 6.1 Location of fragments of the Athenian Decree on Coinage, Weights, and Measures

Decree Enforcing the Use of Athenian Coinage, Weights, and Measures

IG I^3 1453 with additions, O&R 155, *AIO*, *TN* 78. Translation largely following those of O&R and *AIO*. Bold numbers in parentheses indicate clauses.

(**1**) – – – – in the cities, or magistrates(?) – – – – – – –

(**2**) The *Hellenotamiai* are to – – – – – – – – – –magistrates are to make a record; and if anyone disputes(?) – – – – – – of any of the cities, the *Hellenotamiai* are (?) to bring them(?) to the lawcourt of the *thesmothetai* according to the law. And the *thesmothetai* are to – – – – – – – – – – each. (**3**) If anyone (?) apart from(?) the magistrates in the cities does not act in accordance with what has been decreed, either citizens or foreigners, let him lose his civic rights and let his property be confiscated and a tithe of it be given to the goddess. (**4**) And if there are no Athenian magistrates – – – – – – – – – – the magistrates of each city are to do what is prescribed in the decree. And if they do not act in accordance with what is decreed – – – – – – – – – – – – these concerning loss(?) of civic rights – – – – – – – – – – – – (**5**) And in the mint, the silver – – – – – – – – – not less than half, and– – – – – – – – – – – – – the cities act – – – – – – – – – drachmas from the min[a – – – – – – – – – –exchange, or be liable according to the law. (**6**) And whatever silver is left over – – – – – – – – – – – – – – either to the generals or – – – – – – – – – – – – – – – Whenever it is handed over– – – – – – – – – – – to Athena and Hephaistos – – – – – And if anyone makes or puts to a vote a proposal about these things – – – – – to use or lend for some other purpose let him immediately be led off to the Eleven; and the Eleven are to punish him with death; and if he disputes the charge let them bring him to court. (**7**) And the People are to choose heralds to announce what has been decreed, one to the Islands, one to Ionia, one to the Hellespont, one to the Thraceward region; and the generals(?) –– – – – – – – – – – are to dispatch them. If they do not, they are to be fined 10,000 drachmas at their audit. (**8**) And the magistrates are to write up this decree, one in each of the cities. They are to put it on a stone stele in the marketplace at the expense of each city, and the superintendents (of the Athenian mint) are to place it in front of the mint. The Alliance is to carry this out if the magistrates themselves are unwilling. (**9**) And the herald who goes to them is to require them to do all that the Athenians order. (**10**) And the secretary of the *Boule* and the People is to add the following to the oath of the *Boule*:

(*in the Aphytis version*) "If anyone strikes silver coins in the cities or uses coins other than that of the Athenians or weights and measures other than those of the Athenians, I will exact punishment and penalize him."

(**11–12**) (*appended to the Smyrna version*) According to the former decree which Klearchos proposed – – – – – – – – – – the foreign silver – – – – – – – – – – – – – – – – – whenever he wishes; and the city – – – – – – – – – – – – – each his own– – – – – – – – – – [to] the mint. And the superintendents (of the mint)– – – – – – – – – – – – – – – – having written up, are to deposit (or, set up?) – – – – – – – in front of the mint for anyone who wishes to examine; [and they shall write up the total of] foreign (coinage), separately – silver – – –.

The body of the decree that is preserved begins with a directive that the *Hellenotamiai* are to record information that was previously mentioned; goes on to specify procedures and penalties for magistrates, citizens, and even foreigners in the cities who do not comply with the implementation of the decree; and then (in clause 5) turns to a new topic: what is to be done at the mint in Athens.

Here we find mostly large gaps in the text and only a few isolated words which nevertheless have led scholars to deduce that the section mandated the striking of allied cities' silver coinage that was to be sent to Athens into Athenian coinage, at least half of it right away. As a minting charge, a certain number of drachmas were to be deducted from every mina (100 drachmas) of Athenian coins struck. Although the commonly accepted restoration of the text at this point requires that the fee was either three or five drachmas per mina, the higher figure is almost certainly right, since, as one commentator observes, "this would be about the same fee that would have been charged by a money changer for exchanging one kind of coin for another" (Melville Jones, *TN*.2, 69), and because the fee must have been quite profitable. This we infer from a time of financial crisis in the mid-fourth century when the Athenians devalued and then reminted all of their existing coinage for the sole purpose of raising revenue from the minting fee (Kroll 2011a). In the present decree we see that the minting was expected to provide substantial income as well if it was to be the source of the surplus money that would be forwarded to the generals and (probably as a tithe of the total) to Athena and Hephaistos, the guardian deities of metal-workers and the mint. We read further that the accumulated fund of these two gods was to be protected by the threat of the death penalty. (It is unclear what about the funds needed such protection, but it is reminiscent of the "iron reserve," which was safeguarded by the penalty of death for anyone who even proposed to use it for anything other than its dedicated purpose, in that case, emergency funding in the event of a naval attack on Athens [Thuc. 2.24; cf. 8.15]).

There follow regulations for sending out the decree to the four administrative districts of the *arche* and for setting up a copy inscribed on a stone stele in every city and by the superintendents of the mint in Athens in front of the mint. In one fragment (the second Aphytis fragment), it appears that final responsibility for completion of all of these arrangements was delegated to the corporate body of Athens' allies.

The decree's command-and-control impositions themselves are not so surprising in comparison with other legislation concerning the *arche*. But the decree ends, in the Aphytis version, with an extraordinary provision of enforcement: an addition to the oath annually sworn by the 500 members of the *Boule*. The addition holds them responsible for compliance with the core terms of the decree, which, in a sweeping ban, forbids cities from minting their own coinage and any use of non-Athenian coinage, weights, and measures. The insertion of this addition to the oath makes clear that opposition may have been expected not only from the cities but also from Athenians serving in the *Boule* (and as mentioned earlier, the *Boule* had oversight of much of Athens' financial operations).

Two fundamental difficulties, however, arise. The first is the seemingly impossible burden that the decree's formulation created for Athens and the allies alike by failing to distinguish between large-denomination and fractional currency. The decree appears to order a blanket ban on non-Athenian coinage. Any such ban on silver coinage, however, would have required Athens to provide literally millions of small denomination coins to its member states, which would have been solely for internal use, to replace the circulating currency. We should not underestimate the profit motive driving this measure, through which the Athenians stood to gain a one-time windfall in minting fees. But small change would not contribute to these profits because of the high cost of minting such tiny pieces in huge volumes. So, it could well be that the framers of the decree were thinking only of larger unit coins, local coins of, say, a drachma or more in value, and had reason to think that the magistrates in the allied cities would understand this as well (Kroll 2013, 114n26). But, equally, they may not have. It is easy for us to see the impracticability of the replacement of small change. Yet, however obvious to us, looking at the ban from the outside and in hindsight, we should not assume that the Athenians were thinking along the same lines. After all, not all of their legislative decisions made practical sense. Examples ridiculed in comedy, are decrees regarding a salt tax, the bronze coinage, and a certain 2 1/2 percent tax that in the play is presented as a fiasco (Aristophanes, *Eccl.* 815–29).

The second difficulty concerns cities that minted in large denominations partly for the purpose of trade outside the *arche*. An excellent example is the cluster of cities situated along the northern rim of the Aegean – Thasos, Abdera, Maroneia, and Ainos – that conducted their inland trade with the Thracian hinterland in their own regionally familiar coinages. Any prohibition on the production and use of these coinages would have had a disrupting impact on the cities' commerce outside the limits of the Athenian *arche*. We should keep in mind a fundamental fact about the Athenians' motivation behind this enactment: it was ultimately for the benefit to Athens, and not intended to interfere with their allies' ability to produce revenue, from wherever it came.

Now let us return to the discrepancies among the fragments, some of which we noted were important. Recent analyses of the fragments have persuaded some scholars (notably Matthaiou 2009, 171–87; and Stroud 2006, 26) that some belong to a second version of the decree, in which the oath of the *Boule* reads as follows:

> If anyone strikes silver coins in the cities and does not use the coins of the Athenians or their weights or measures, but foreign coins and weights and measures, [I will punish him].

In contrast to the oath known from the Aphytis fragment, this one, pieced together from several fragments, most critically the one from Olbia, and with it the fragment seen at Smyrna, would seem to allow the allies to mint a coinage of their own, so long as they also use Athenian coins, weights, and measures (Figueira 1998, 394). This notion that the two versions of the oath were purposefully and substantively different from one another, however, has been questioned by scholars who prefer to see the variations in the wording of the oath (and in a few lesser words or phrases) as the result of casualness in the reproduction of multiple copies for distribution and inscribing throughout the empire (O&R 155, *AIO*). The matter remains under discussion, but it is difficult to will away this discrepancy. If we do not insist on a single position regarding the use of non-Athenian coinage, we stand to learn much about what may have been a real shift in thinking in the *Boule* and assembly.

Indeed, another indication of at least two phases in the legislation comes from the Smyrna fragment, which continues with at least nine (we lack the end of this version of the decree) further, and very broken, lines of text (clauses 11 and 12) following the oath. (The Siphnos fragment also continues beyond the oath, though what followed in that portion of the decree is not extant.) These lines reproduce a certain "former decree of Klearchos," which evidently specified that anyone "whenever he wishes" could bring foreign money to the Athenian mint for recoining. Among other things, this decree required the superintendents of the mint to record the amount of foreign coinage received and to display the total in front of the mint. Despite the loss of so much procedural detail, we infer that the Athenian mint was free to coin and profit from any money that was brought in *voluntarily* for conversion to Attic coin. We would like to know whether this was a new or recent policy or whether it had already been in effect for some time and was only added to the alternative version of the Decree on Coinage, Weights, and Measures for the purpose of clarification. Because this version of the decree appears to address certain difficulties presented in the original decree, it would have been issued relatively soon after the promulgation of the original one. If we understand it correctly, the provision in the Klearchos fragment, along with the mandates in the other fragments, is nothing short of revolutionary: the Athenians, in constructing a new economic union, were not only ordering cities in their empire to conform to their standards and coinage but also facilitating the participation of private individuals. In doing so the state mint assumed the role of private *trapezetai* (money-changers) for obtaining Athenian silver. (An invitation, not an order, to participate is paralleled by the clause in the "First Fruits" Eleusis decree [O&R 141, *AIO*] in which, in addition to mandating that cities within the *arche* bring first fruits to Eleusis, other Greeks are invited to do so as well.)

The coinage part of the decree deserves to be put in perspective. As we observed in Chapter 2, because of their massively increasing volume and privileged status within the Athenian *arche*, the employment of Athenian tetradrachms had become widespread throughout the empire prior to the passage of the decree. Hence the decree, it seems, would have served to complete by force of law a monetary phenomenon that had long been developing. By making the use of Athenian coinage mandatory, the chief target of the decree in its original form would have been those relatively few but economically significant cities that were still using a large-denomination coinage of their own more or less exclusively, and certainly in the collection of harbor taxes. These included the several minting cities along the Thracian coast mentioned earlier, as well as some of the wealthier cities of the Eastern Aegean, such as Samos and Chios.

Attic-Standard Weights at Olympia and Kyzikos

But what about Athenian weights and measures? Had their use, too, been spreading prior to the enactment of the decree? In fact, evidence for this has been found outside the *arche* in the harvest of nearly 300 fifth- and fourth-century bronze balance weights that were excavated in and around the Sanctuary of Zeus at Olympia (Hitzl 1996). Inscribed with the name of Zeus, these weights were the property of the sanctuary, which evidently rented them out to merchants at the great festival market and vendors of food and other goods for the spectators. The first large group of these weights consisted of those that were adjusted to the Aeginetan weight standard (mina of 70 Aeginetan drachmas = 435 g), the nearly universal standard of the Peloponnese, as one would expect at a Peloponnesian festival managed by the city of Elis (p. 92).

Added to these later in the century, however, was a second group of weights based on the uniquely Athenian commercial standard mina of 105 Athenian drachmas (= 457 g; see Appendix A.2). The intriguing introduction of these Attic weights (Fig. 6.4) can scarcely be attributed to any time in the fifth century other than the year 420 (Kroll 1998), when, soon after the Peace of Nikias was sworn, Athens entered into negotiations with Elis and two other Peloponnesian states, Argos and Mantineia, which also had grievances with Sparta, and concluded with them a mutual defensive alliance (Thuc. 5.47; O&R 165; *AIO*). As tensions between Sparta and Elis escalated, the Elians banned Sparta from participating in the Olympic festival that summer and held the games under the protection of

Figure 6.4 Bronze balance weight from the Sanctuary of Zeus at **Olympia** (420– *c.* 380 BC). Four minas (1832 g) on the Attic trade standard. Inscribed ΔΙΟΣ ("Of Zeus," i.e., "Belonging to Zeus"). The letter *chi* below was added to Attic-standard weights, to distinguish them from similarly shaped weights at Olympia on the Aeginetan standard. Hitzl 1996, 158, no. 14.

an armed force including some Athenian cavalry in the event of Spartan interference (Thuc. 5.49–50). Presumably, in the negotiations and mutual good will that led to this new alliance, the Athenians obtained from the Elians a concession that, in addition to the traditional Aeginetan ones, the weight and measurement standards of Athens would be made available also for use at the festival market that accompanied the games.

These standards are a clear result of politics, a manifestation of the changed diplomatic relationship between Athens and Elis, traditionally a member of the Peloponnesian League. But the practical effect was economic: the concession conferred acceptance of Athenian commercial standards at the largest and most prestigious Panhellenic festival in the Greek world. This would have made the festival market more welcoming to merchants from the commercial network of the Athenian *arche*, potentially expanding it. The very fact that the Athenians raised this concession regarding the instruments of festival trade while arranging a major military alliance with the Elians is a forceful reminder of the importance of commerce in Athenian thinking at this time of peace.

Besides these Attic-standard weights at Olympia, there survive two nearly identical lead balance weights from the city of Kyzikos on this same trade standard (Kroll 2018). Both weigh one-quarter of an Athenian commercial mina (*c.* 115 g) and display an owl with the olive-leaf sprig, as copied from fifth-century Athenian tetradrachms, standing on a tunafish, the civic badge of Kyzikos (Fig. 6.5). In light of the propagation of Athenian weights and measures at Olympia in 420 BC, it is conceivable that Kyzikos might independently have adopted the Athenian weight standard before

Figure 6.5 Lead balance weight of **Kyzikos** (414–404 BC). 115 g (= one-quarter of a mina on the Attic trade standard). An Athenian owl, with an olive sprig behind its head, stands on a tunafish, the state emblem of Kyzikos. The retrograde letters pi-omicron to the right of the owl's legs are an abbreviation of poleōs ("of the city") certifying that the weight was an official weight of the city. Oxford, Ashmolean Museum, Inv. 1996.306.

such adoption was mandated in the Coinage, Weights, and Measures Decree(s). But the way the Kyzikene weights were manufactured suggests that they probably were a response to the mandate. Whereas Greek weights were normally made by casting molten metal in square molds, these Kyzikene weights were produced by stamping the design into preweighed lead blocks, a much faster, mass-production technique that was especially well suited for turning out hundreds of new balance weights as quickly as possible in order to comply with the decree. No similar Athenian-standard weights are known from other cities in the *arche*, but the Kyzikene examples are evidence enough that the Coins, Weights, and Measures Decree had moved beyond the publication of the law in the cities' market-places to its implementation: at least one city made up and used new weights on the Athenian standard that were visibly identified as such by the owl device of Athenian coins.

The Coinage, Weights, and Measures Decree and the *Eikoste*: Success or Failure?

We have mentioned earlier (p. 24) the possibility that the part of the decree that seems to detail the mass restriking of allied coins into Athenian coinage may have been responsible for the hurried, hence substandard, die-cutting that characterizes a large bloc of late Standardized owls that probably date from around this time. Currently, however, we lack any evidence for the impact of the decree on the minting of local coinages – and not only because a second version of the decree may have allowed local minting if a city also used Athenian coins. Even without that interpretation of two contrasting versions of the bouleutic oath, the decree could only have taken effect when, within two years, Athens' power was shaken by the disaster in Sicily and the subsequent outbreaks of revolts among its allies, assisted by a new Spartan fleet. In these changed conditions, implementation and enforcement of the decree would have become erratic at best and hence potentially moot. Even so, we should not lose sight of the fact that, as conceived, it was a far-reaching enactment and, as possibly modified, flexible enough to exempt coinages that were oriented to networks beyond the *arche*.

The fate of the *eikoste* itself is unknown. Many scholars believe that it was soon abandoned as Athens' primary instrument of revenue and that tribute was restored, inasmuch as Xenophon (*Hell.* 1.3.9) mentions an agreement dating to 408 whereby the city of Kalchedon would pay to the Athenians "the tribute it was accustomed to paying, plus what it already owed." Nevertheless, if we can use Aristophanes as evidence, an *eikostologos* (a collector of the 5 percent tax), was in place in Aegina's harbor as late as 405 (*Frogs*, line 363), implying that the Athenians continued to collect the harbor duties at certain cities at least. Moreover, after Athens' loss of empire in 404, the *eikoste* emerges as a tax imposed by Thrasyboulos around 390 BC at Klazomenai and Thasos (R&O 18; *IG* II^2 24.a.3–6), during a campaign to restore Athens' hegemony in the Aegean. Might he have been one of the brains behind the earlier decision to abolish tribute, impose an *arche*-wide tax, and possibly to create a coinage and metrological union throughout the *arche*?

7

The Ionian War and Loss of Empire, 413–404 BC

Athens after 413

Athens' and Sparta's respective worlds changed radically in the winter of 413. The Athenians' attempt to conquer Syracuse, and with that, as noted in the previous chapter, the expedition was shortly to end in catastrophe, especially when a Spartan detachment to Sicily to help the Syracusans proved pivotal in the war. Also in 413 the Spartans installed a permanent fort at Dekeleia in northern Attica. This directly threatened the mining industry at Laureion, but instead of withdrawing from the Sicilian campaign in order to face the new threats at home, the Athenians pressed on when reinforcements arrived from Athens. (We noted in Thucydides' mention of the *eikoste* [p. 107], his gripping account of the Athenians' determination to proceed now with two wars.) In Sicily, however, the Athenians met with utter defeat.

> *It was, as they say, total annihilation. Beaten in every way on every front, extreme miseries suffered on an extreme scale, and army, fleet, and everything else, destroyed. Few out of many made their return home.* (Thuc. 7.87.6, trans. Hammond, abridged)

The "everything else" included the loss of money. Thucydides comments on the Athenians' surrender to the Syracusans and its impact at home: "*they lost hoplites, cavalry and troops and did not see any left to replace them; but when they saw, too, that there were no ships in their docks, or money in the treasury, or crews, they were in a state of despair*" (Thuc. 8.1.2).

The victorious Syracusans, in turn, were enriched by their capture of the men and their money. It has been argued that the spectacular coins Syracuse issued in the last third of the fifth century (see Fig. 7.1) were connected with money from the sale of Athenian captives (whether through slavery or ransoming) and the cash and other spoils seized from the Athenians, including the lavish equipment the Athenians had brought with them (Thuc. 6.31). If so, it is attractive to see the coinage, given its unsurpassed artistry, beginning as a victory coinage (Carnevaro and Rutter 2014).

Figure 7.1 Silver tetradrachm of **Syracuse** (413–*c.* 400 BC), after the defeat of the Athenian expedition. Similar to earlier Syracusan tetradrachms (as Fig. 6.3) but with dies executed by the far more sophisticated die-engraver, Euainetos, who depicts the chariot group in a three-quarter perspective racing at full speed. The chariot wheel lying in the space below, the result of an accident, and the loose rein (of the far horse) dropping on the ground, emphasize the excitement and danger of the event. The coin was inscribed on both sides: in addition to the ethnic ΣΥΡΑΚΟΣΙΟΝ above the head of Arethusa on the reverse, the engraver signed his name ΕΥΑΙΝΕΤΟ in tiny letters on the ground line on the obverse. Owing to wear on the die and this coin, the signature has almost entirely disappeared; it is known from better preserved specimens from the same die. Attic standard. 17.28 g. *ANS.*
Euainetos was one of ten master die-engravers employed by Syracuse in the years following the city's victory over the Athenians, an era known to numismatists as "the period of the signing artists" and admired for the visual brilliance of their signed coins. Syracuse's patronage of these master artists, who must have commanded the highest engraving fees in the Greek world, is an indication of how greatly the city profited from ransoms and booty produced by the Athenian defeat (Canevaro and Rutter 2014).

Yet, in the immediate aftermath of the Sicilian debacle, instead of wholesale collapse as might have been expected, the Athenians were able to rebuild their fleet, to exercise prudence in domestic expenditure, and to take the unprecedented step of appointing a board of ten elders who would have a supervisory role in limiting debate in the democracy (Thuc. 8.3). Conventionally, we call the war in what turned out to be the final stage of the Peloponnesian War, the "Dekeleian War" – because of the Spartans' full-time presence in Attica; or the "Ionian War," because of the theater of war that took place in Ionia and off its coast. It was here that the Spartans devoted their efforts in order to break up the *arche*, finally in recognition that in order to win the war they had to overpower Athens at sea. But this strategic shift would create enormous financial challenges of its own, for both sides.

As mentioned earlier, the Spartan fort, in addition to cutting off access to land and homes in Attica, greatly curtailed if it did not shut down altogether the silver-mining industry at Laureion. Slaves on which the industry depended took advantage of the Spartan presence to escape, and by rendering the Attic countryside insecure, the large-scale processing and smelting of ore that took place in the open would have been difficult if not impossible to sustain (p. 25). However much revenue the mining industry had produced for the city of Athens in rents, taxes, and minting, the loss or near loss of this industry to the public and private economy of Athens was not negligible.

Athens' external revenue was also in decline. In 412, in panic upon the revolt of the island polity of Chios, previously a staunch ally, the Athenians took the dramatic step of releasing their thousand talent "iron reserve" – this, as mentioned earlier (p. 116), had been earmarked solely for use in the event of a naval attack on Athens. The release of this reserve, and probably also the 100 ships set aside with it (Thuc. 2.24), is clear testimony to their financial insecurity, which only increased with a near-domino effect as more cities in the eastern Aegean revolted with the support of the energized Spartan fleet. Besides Chios, these included Erythrai, Klazomenai, Teos, Ephesos, Miletos, Iasos, and the major island of Rhodes. Closer to home, the Athenians were especially devastated by the revolt in 411 of Euboea; this large island just off Attica had been a primary source of grain and other agricultural provisions during the war. At Athens, after a bloody oligarchic coup of some 400 men in that year, the Athenians deposed them and instituted a moderate oligarchy before restoring the democracy soon after. Instability, both domestic and financial, characterize these years.

Financing the Spartan Fleet

Let us turn to the Spartan side. We begin with the question: how were the Spartans able to finance a fleet? Already in 413, King Agis assigned quotas to Sparta's allies for building a hundred new ships – along with making plain extortions of money from them (Thuc. 8.3). These efforts, however, did not come close to raising the necessary financing for the continuous manning of a full fleet. We have also noted the non-monetary contributions listed in the Spartan war fund inscription, whatever its precise date (p. 90); if typical, this practice would have been inadequate over the longer term, given the Spartans' need to raise regular monetary funds. (Recall the comments attributed to the Spartan king, Archidamos, about the Spartans' lack of financial reserves, p. 90). For the Spartans, then, external financing for their fleet was critical.

Enter the Persians. Darius II, Great King since the late 420s, had his own agenda, namely, to recover the Greek cities on the Asiatic coast and islands that were historically an important source of tribute until they joined the Athenian empire. Indeed, the successive Persian Kings (Artaxerxes and Darius) may never have formally accepted Athens' possession of these cities, and thus would have demanded tribute from them. Whenever this occurred, however, the burden fell on the King's satraps to produce revenue in the form of tribute. Thucydides provides a glimpse of the pressure on satraps in the later stages of the Peloponnesian War. Following the Sicilian disaster, two satraps, Tissaphernes and Pharnabazos, were being pressed by the King to produce overdue tribute (Thuc. 8.6). If Sparta defeated Athens and broke up its empire, the cities would revert to Persia (as the thinking went – in fact, Sparta claimed a number of these cities after the war ended).

The Spartans and the Persians made several treaties acknowledging in no uncertain terms the King's claims on the cities in Asia. They failed, however, to address sufficiently the Persians' financing of Sparta's war against Athens: the Spartans were eager for Persian financial backing, yet the treaties are fairly opaque about the actual monetary and other commitments promised for this stage of the war. The Spartans had to search for crumbs of funding until 407, when Cyrus, the King's son, was sent to the front with special authority to finance the Spartan navy (and to return the Asiatic cities to the Persian empire). Cyrus found Lysander, the Spartan general then on the scene, to be someone he could trust, and straightaway produced 500 talents; after that was used up, he continued to bankroll the navy when Lysander again assumed command a year later (Xen. *Hell.* 1.4.1–3, 5.1–3; 2.1.10–14).

Coins and the Spartan Fleet

In assessing the eventual Spartan victory in a prospective passage early on his work, Thucydides (2.65.12) signals the importance of Persian financing of the Spartan side in explaining its defeat of Athens (though he believed that internal factionalism among the Athenians was the overriding factor). The central point, however, was clear: whereas money made the Athenian empire, it would be money that would bring it down. In Thucydides' and Xenophon's accounts of negotiations between Greeks and Persian satraps over pay, the money is expressed in Athenian minas, drachmas, and obols (Thuc. 8.29.1, 8.45.2; Xen. *Hell.* 1.5.4). Although it might be tempting to think that these Athenian writers are expressing pay in their own, familiar currency, this is less likely, since, as mentioned in Chapter 2 (pp. 33–4), the

a.   b.

Figure 7.2 Persian royal coinages (fifth and fourth centuries BC). (**a**) Persian gold daric. Babylonian shekel (8.35 g) standard. On the obverse the Persian hero-king is shown crowned and running, carrying a spear and bow. The reverse consists of a simple rectangular punch. 8.31 g. *ANS*. Darics, the only continuously minted coinage of pure gold during the fifth century, were named after King Darius I, who introduced them in the late sixth century. The common type shown here continued to be minted without change for almost two centuries. (**b**) Silver siglos with the same obverse and reverse types, but minted on the Persian siglos (5.5 g) standard. 5.37 g. *ANS*.

Persians had accumulated stocks of Attic owls, and even had begun to mint imitations of them, making it unexceptional that a great many Persian naval subventions during the Ionian War were probably disbursed in Athenian coinage (Thompson 1964, 122). For their part, rowers in the Peloponnesian fleet, most of them mercenaries from around the Greek world, were accustomed to being paid in Greek currency, which at this time in the Aegean meant Athenian owls.

Spartan financing at this time involved other coinages as well. Sums specifically in Aeginetan staters and in Persian gold darics are recorded in the Spartan war fund inscription (p. 91). Scholarly opinion is divided whether the contributions in the list began in the 420s or belong entirely to the time of the Ionian War (O&R, pp. 298–300), but in either case it is clear that the most significant sums in the inscription were those paid in Persian darics because of the gold coins' high value (at this time one daric was worth twenty-three Attic drachmas). Although darics (Fig. 7.2a) had been minted by Persian kings since the end of the sixth century, they seem not to have circulated widely in Aegean Greece until late in the Peloponnesian War when Darius II and his satraps in western Asia Minor lent their backing to the Spartan cause. A payment in darics mentioned by Thucydides (8.28.4) dates to 412, when the Peloponnesian fleet seized the city of Iasos, south of Miletos, and received from the satrap Tissaphernes one daric for each captive taken. So prized internationally were these fine coins of pure gold that by the later fifth century many were passing into private savings and the public treasuries of Athens (pp. 42–3).

In contrast, the similarly designed silver coin of the Persians, the siglos (Fig. 7.2b), hardly ever circulated outside of western Asia Minor. For most of the fifth century the Persians employed these two coinages in a bimetallic system in which twenty silver sigloi were equivalent to a daric. Owing to shifts in the availability and relative values of gold and silver toward the end of the century, however, this fixed sigloi-to-daric ratio could no longer be maintained, and the Persian authorities, whose accounting was based on gold, abandoned the minting and use of sigloi and chose in their dealings with Greeks to employ silver coinages of Greek mintage instead (Carradice 1987, 92–3; Ellis-Evans and Kagan forthcoming).

Thus, while the Spartans relied largely on the coinages of Persian gold and Athenian and Aeginetan silver during this last phase of the war, other Greek silver coinages were enlisted as needed, especially the coinage of Chios, the island that served from time to time as a base and source of ad hoc funding for the Spartan fleet. Before leaving Chios in 411, the Spartan admiral Mindaros obtained from the Chians a payment of three "fortieths" (as they are called by Thucydides [8.101.1]) for each of his sailors. It is now recognized that these were coins worth a fortieth of a gold daric and were in fact the silver "thirds" that the Chians had been routinely minting for some time (Fig. 3.22b; Ellis-Evans 2016, 9–10; Hardwick 1996). What emerges clearly is that these local Chian coins were now being identified by their value in darics, no better sign of just how readily the Spartans and their new Greek allies embraced the bimetallic Persian accounting system based on gold. The Persian daric had become their chief coin of reference.

At some later point, the Chians switched to minting fourths or drachmas (Fig. 7.3a) of a new double-weight stater, which now became a tetradrachm (Fig. 7.3b). One result of these changed denominations was to make Chian silver readily exchangeable with both the Aeginetan-weight coinage of Sparta's allies (8 Chian drachmas = 5 Aeginetan) and the Persian silver siglos (3 Chian drachmas = 2 sigloi); another was the convenience of the larger Chian coins for the ever-larger expenditures needed by Spartan commanders. In a recent discussion (Ellis-Evans 2016, 7–12), the shifts to the larger coin units are dated to the year 406, when the Chians first provided the Spartan admiral Kallikratidas with a five-drachma stipend for every man under his command – a one-off payment – and later in the year, in order to avoid an insurrection, were persuaded by another commander to buy off the unpaid and starving personnel of the Peloponnesian fleet stationed on Chios with a full month's stipend per sailor (Xen. *Hell.* 2.1.5 with 1.6.12). As these episodes involving occasional payments of

a.   b.

Figure 7.3 Silver drachma and tetradrachm of **Chios** (*c.* 406 BC). Chian standard. Although both coins continue the earlier types of Chios (Fig. 3.22) – obverse seated sphinx before an amphora and bunch of grapes and reverse of a square divided into quarters – the old denominational units of staters and thirds were replaced with new denominations, a tetradrachm (of doubled, or full, 15.6 g stater weight) divided into four drachmas (of 3.9 g). The obverse field of the drachma (**a**) is plain. 3.59 g. *ANS.* The tetradrachm (**b**) has a wreath of grape leaves encircling the sphinx. 15.33 g. *Vienna. Schottenstift.*

Figure 7.4 Electrum stater of **Chios** (*c.* 406/5 BC). Chian standard. The vine wreath around the sphinx relates this exceptional Chian issue of electrum to the Chian tetradrachm in Fig. 7.3b. The stater's reverse imitates the reverse incuse square design of Kyzikene electrum staters (see Fig. 3.1). 15.33 g. *Berlin.*

Chian silver to Spartan naval commanders underscore, the Spartans' ability to maintain a fleet was precarious before Lysander finally took command.

In addition to these new silver denominations, the Chians minted an exceptional but limited coinage of electrum staters (Fig. 7.4; Hardwick 1993, 213–16), which may also have been needed for pay for the fleet, unless they were intended for Lysander's program of ship building in early 405 (Ellis-Evans 2016, 7–12). The recent association of two other fine electrum coinages of Chian or near-Chian weight with the Spartan war effort (Ellis-Evans 2016) is, however, problematic. One of these is the final issue of the long, but intermittent, series of staters from Lampsakos (Fig. 7.6), which had been a Troad weight coinage since its archaic beginnings (pp. 43–4). The other is known from a single surviving stater of Mytilene (Fig. 7.5), whose weight might actually reflect alignment with the electrum of Lampsakos rather than with coinage of Chios. The fact that both Mytilene and Lampsakos were subject to Athens for all but a few days or weeks during the last decade of the war raises further questions

Figure 7.5 Electrum stater of **Mytilene** (late fifth century BC). Chian standard. The obverse head of Apollo, wearing a wreath of laurel leaves, is similar to the head of the god on earlier drachmas of the city (Fig. 5.3b). Here the abbreviated ethnic MYTI was placed on the obverse, perhaps to ensure that the coin would not be mistaken for a (slightly heavier) electrum stater of Kyzikos. The reverse punch replicates those of Kyzikene staters. 15.44 g. *London.*

Figure 7.6 Electrum stater of **Lampsakos** (late fifth century BC). Troad standard. This stater (15.15 g, *ANS*) with the small letter *xi* beneath the winged horse in a wreath belongs to the very last issue of the Lampsakene electrum (see Fig. 3.2). It is one of about twenty uncirculated examples, all from the same obverse die, in a large hoard from ancient Klazomenai (Appendix B, no. 35) along with electrum staters of Kyzikos and Persian darics; the date of the hoard (*c.* 410–400 BC) shows that these lampsakenes were struck relatively late in the century. Hardwick (1993, 213–218) grouped the Chian-weight staters of Chios and Mytilene (Figs. 7.4 and 7.5) together with these lampsakenes, dating them all 412–410 BC. Ellis-Evans (2016) dates them to c. 405/4 as coinages struck in support of Lysander. But it is not certain that they all must be dated together just because of their common weights.

about the role of these particular coinages in the war. What was decisive was Cyrus' unlimited source of money, which guaranteed that Lysander would have all the resources he needed to defeat the Athenian navy (Xen. *Hell.* 1.5.3; 2.1.14).

Emergency Coinages at Athens

From the year 412, when a bloody revolution in Samos brought a popular, pro-Athenian government to power, the island polis became the naval station of the Athenian fleet in the eastern Aegean and remained so down to the end of the Ionian War. The Samians atticized their coinage accordingly. The types and the look of the coinage remained as before (Fig. 3. 23), but the weights of the tetradrachms and their divisions were raised from the

Figure 7.7 Silver tetradrachm of **Samos** (c. 410 BC). Attic standard. The obverse lion scalp and the forepart of a bull on the reverse are continued from the long series of preceding Samian tetradrachms of lower Samian weight (Fig. 3.23). Inscribed above the bull is the abbreviated ethnic, ΣΑΜΙ. The AP monogram beneath is the signature of the responsible magistrate. 16.84 g. *ANS*.

Samian standard (13.1 g) to the Attic (17.2 g) for the four issues between 412 and 404 (Fig. 7.7). While this shift to coining on the Attic standard was not without political overtones, from a practical standpoint it was a measure for provisioning the Athenian fleet and simplifying exchange with the exceptional amount of Athenian money that must have entered the public and private economy of Samos at the time.

Thanks in large part to the thousand talents freed up from the "iron reserve," Athens was able to afford the cost of maintaining a sizable fleet at sea for a couple of years, but by 409 cash reserves in the form of minted silver had been depleted and the city was forced to turn to its next store of precious metal, namely, the dedications in silver and gold on the Acropolis. We know this from the annually inscribed inventories. Some of the objects disappear from these lists, no doubt because they had been requisitioned and melted down for coining, a practice explicitly attested in an ancient commentary on a famous passage in Aristophanes' *Frogs*. The commentary informs us that in the year 407/6 the Athenians minted a gold coinage from the gold statues of Nike, the goddess of Victory, and then in the next year minted a bronze coinage. In the *Frogs* itself, which was produced in the middle of 406/5 and won first prize, Aristophanes' chorus makes reference to three Athenian coinages – the old silver coinage, the new gold coinage, and a base coinage of bronze that had just been introduced. This part of the play falls within the *parabasis*, in which the poet (in the voice of the Chorus Leader) traditionally addresses the Athenian audience, urging them to improve their ways. Here, Aristophanes likens the good and base coinages to good and bad politicians (lines 718–26):

> *The city often seems to us to treat*
> *the finest and noblest of its citizens*
> *the same way that it has treated the old coinage and the new gold.*

Figure 7.8 Gold coinage of **Athens** (407–404 BC). Attic standard. (**a**) Didrachm stater, 8.61 g. *NAC*. (**b**) Drachma or half-stater, 4.30 g. *Berlin*. (**c**) Triobol or quarter-stater, 2.16 g. *London*. (**d**) Diobol or third-stater, 1.43 g. *ANS*. (**e**) Obol or sixth-stater, 0.72 g. *ANS*.

> *Those coins are not debased,*
> *but the finest of all coins, it is agreed,*
> *the only ones that are stamped honestly and ring true,*
> *among the Greeks and the barbarians everywhere.*
> *Yet we don't use them, but instead these vile bronze ones*
> *that were coined just yesterday or the day before, in a really bad strike.*

From contemporary inscribed inventories originally displayed on the Acropolis, we know that there were eight gold statues of Nike housed in the Parthenon, each made with two talents of gold that were cast in pieces and attached to an iron armature for easy removal; seven of these statues were dismantled, melted, and turned into coin, the last in 405/404 (Thompson 1970). From the fourteen talents of gold that were coined, about thirty coins survive today. They occur in five denominations (Fig. 7.8a–e): the stater (weight of two silver drachmas), the one-drachma half-stater, the triobol quarter-stater, the diobol third-stater, and the obol sixth. A fifth denomination, the hemiobol twelfth, is known from an inscribed inventory (*IG* II^2 1414, 6). The types are the same as used for Athenian silver coins, with the addition on reverses of an olive branch on the stem of which the owl stands. On the gold triobol (Fig. 7.8c) the owl is framed by two branches, which, instead of hanging down from above as on silver triobols, rise up, again, from under the owl's feet.

Since the coins were valued at a gold:silver ratio of 1:12, the largest of the gold coins, the stater, would have been worth six silver tetradrachms and the smallest, the hemiobol, a silver drachma. These then were high-value coins destined primarily for spending abroad, in the first instance, for the construction of ships with Macedonian timber that were authorized very probably in 407/6 (O&R 188, *AIO*; Thompson 1966). When judged by past military expenditures, the fourteen talents of gold from the Nikai were a relatively modest sum, the equivalent of only 168 talents of silver. But we should remember that, in the event of a more protracted war, the Athenians still had, in addition to one more gold Nike, forty talents of gold (the equivalent of 480 talents of silver) that could be removed from the statue of Athena in the Parthenon, which at the start of the war Perikles had singled out as a reserve of last resort (Thuc. 2.13.5) – and which, much later, the Athenian general and tyrant Lachares actually did employ for minting a gold coinage when Athens was under siege in 295 BC (Kroll 2011a, 251–4).

When the chorus of *Frogs* laments that Athenians were no longer using the gold and their old silver coins but only a brand new coinage of bronze, we have to allow for comic exaggeration. But the implication is clear: the bronze coins were minted for domestic use in order to free up gold and silver for public expenditure primarily overseas. But which bronze coins were they? They can hardly have been the very small Athenian bronze tokens that some scholars had identified as the *kollyboi* mentioned in passages in Old Comedy from the late 420s (see the passage of Eupolis, p. 149). A *kollybos* was a minuscule value of Athenian weight – one-eighth of a silver obol (0.09 g, to be exact) – that, like the very large weight units of minas and talents [p. 149] was a notional unit and at the time of the comic passages did not exist in the form of a minted coin (Kroll 2015).* Salamis minted bronze coins from sometime in the 430s (p. 88), which makes it doubtful that the reference in *Frogs* to bronze coins "just struck yesterday or the day before" could allude to them.

The one coinage that can be identified with these "vile bronzes" of Aristophanes' chorus is a currency of Athenian bronze coins that were clad with a thin silver veneer to make them resemble silver. From the early days of Greek coinage private counterfeiters frequently employed this ruse of

---

* The small bronze tokens that have sometimes been identified as *kollyboi* are too late to go with the passages. Dating from the fourth century and, mostly, Hellenistic times, more than 600 varieties are known. Like the great number of other Athenian bronze, lead, and clay tokens, they probably served as voucher tokens or admission tickets (Kroll 2015; Lang and Crosby 1963, 84).

a.

b.

c.

d.

e.

Figure 7.9 Plated bronze coinage of **Athens** (406–404 BC). (**a, b**) Tetradrachms: 14.32 and 15.48 g. *Athens, Numismatic Museum.* (**c, d, e**) Drachmas: 2.71, 3.09, and 3.04 g. *ANS.* All of these coins come from the 1902 Piraeus hoard of plated drachmas and tetradrachms (Kroll 1996) and have lost some of their silver veneer from flaking; on most, spots of green corrosion from the bronze core have broken through to the surface.

silver-plating bronze cores to make forgeries. But since the 1902 discovery of a hoard in the Piraeus of over a thousand silver-clad Athenian coins of the same style as the gold coins of 407–404, it has been recognized that the hoard (Appendix B, no. 5a) was in all probability a deposit of the officially struck bronze coinage mentioned in Aristophanes.

The hoard coins (Fig. 7.9; Kroll 1996) had been minted on a large scale with four obverse dies for drachmas and a minimum of two obverse dies for tetradrachms. In addition, plated triobols have been attributed to the coinage. It is doubtful that these plated coins were intended to seriously deceive anyone. After all, the Athenian Assembly had voted to authorize their minting and to mandate their acceptance by law. The coins, moreover, were 15–20 percent lighter than their prototypes in silver, and the bronze cores, when not partially exposed by wear from handling, were easily detected by making a cut along their edge or through the veneer of their surface. Nevertheless, the plating, by giving them a bona fide appearance facilitated the coins' acceptance for the short term during which the coins were expected to serve until, hopefully, better times followed and the coins could be redeemed with coins of pure silver.

It is unclear how the plated coins were issued. One possibility would have been in a forced exchange, whereby everyone was required to exchange their cash in silver for these substitutes. Alternatively, they may have been intended solely for state payments, allowing the city to meet its payrolls to jurors and other domestic obligations with a token currency. In the latter case, the assumption would have been that the plated coins, once paid out, would enter the pool of circulating silver money and be accepted as if they were of good silver; in fact, they would have driven the good silver currency out of circulation into hoarding. But however they were released, their purpose was to conserve as much money of precious metal as was still available to the state for necessary external expenditures. These expenses would have been both military and for the purchase of food, since upon the loss of Euboea, mentioned earlier, the Athenians were obliged to import all of their grain and other products from distant sources.

Seven months after the staging of the *Frogs*, the news reached Athens that the Spartan navy under Lysander's command had surprised and destroyed the Athenian fleet at Aigospotamoi in the Hellespont. Lysander then blockaded Athens by sea, and after eight months the Athenians were starved into surrendering on terms that included the disbanding of all but twelve of their warships, the destruction of their long walls and the fortifications of the Piraeus, and the acceptance of an alliance with Sparta, bringing the war to a close in April 404. By this time all cities of the Athenian empire that had remained within the Athenian orbit had gone over to Sparta, except for Samos, which Lysander besieged and captured some months later.

Aftermath

In a window into the topicality of Old Comedy as well as the preoccupation of Athenians with their money, Aristophanes gives a glimpse of how the bronze coins from the end of the war were "demonetized." In his comedy *Ecclesiazusae* of around 391 BC, two principals, the Citizen and Chremes, reminisce about the ridiculousness of some past Athenian laws, including the legislation about the bronze coins (lines 814–22):

> C. Those bronzes, don't you remember when we voted for them?
>   Ch. Indeed, that turned out to be a bad strike for me. For selling my grapes I went off with my mouth full of bronzes and then came to the market to buy some barley. When I was just holding out my bag, the herald cried out not to accept bronze any longer. "For we are using silver."

a.   b.

Figure 7.10 (**a, b**). Silver tetradrachms of **Athens** (early and mid-fourth century BC). As on all Athenian coins of the fourth century, the face of Athena is more refined than those on Athenian coins of the fifth century. The most distinctive features of the new, fourth-century Athenas are the fully profile eye and more naturally rendered ear. 17.15 g. *ANS*; 17.25 g. *ANS*.

This full return to silver must have followed soon after peace was concluded with Sparta and was made possible by revived state revenues such as port taxes in the Piraeus (Andok. 1.133–4) and, in the private sector, by the availability of precious metal money that had been hoarded, like the silver and gold savings kept by the orator Lysias in the strongbox in his house (p. 47), and presumably in more modest amounts by Athenians of average means. The Athenian mint had begun to strike fresh owls by the late 390s; and the mining industry, hampered by a shortage of slave manpower, got off to a slow new start. Although productivity never approached the scale of Athenian minting in the fifth century, for most of the fourth century Athenian owl silver (Fig. 7.10) maintained its position as the most prolific and abundantly exported coinage in the Aegean world (Kroll 2011b).

In contrast to monetary continuity at Athens, for the cities that had been subjects of Athens, realignment with Sparta brought change: those that coined turned to minting on weight standards congenial to Spartan interests – another narrative not reliant on literary testimony. New silver coinages at Maroneia and Abdera on the Thracian coast and at Mende further to the west were all minted on an unprecedented standard (12.9 g) that was coordinated with the Persian –and now Spartan – money of account, the gold daric (eight of these silver coins being equal in value to the daric [Ellis-Evans and Kagan forthcoming]). But the standard that was commonly adopted by the cities and islands of the eastern Aegean was the Chian, which owed much of its sudden prominence to its compatibility with the Persian siglos and to the extraordinary, politically charged "Alliance" coinage of Chian tridrachms associated with the Spartan commander Lysander.

This is a coinage with a common obverse type depicting the child Herakles strangling two snakes, accompanied by the letters Σ-Υ-Ν, standing for *synmachōn* ("of the allies") or *synmachikon* ("coin of the alliance"). Reverses give the type and in most cases the abbreviated ethnic of the seven cities that are known to have minted the coinage in silver: Ephesos, Samos, Kyzikos, Byzantion, Iasos, Knidos, and Rhodes (Fig. 7.11a–g). An eighth city, Lampsakos, minted the types in a gold issue with the weight of a Persian daric (Fig. 7.12). Hoard evidence (Meadows 2011, 287) fixes this coinage close to the time of Lysander's defeat of Athens, making it credible to identify in the obverse snake-strangling Herakles an allusion to Doric Sparta, if not to Lysander himself (Karwiese 1980), subduing the power of Athens, a city whose goddess Athena and legendary King Kekrops both had strong associations with snakes (Fig. 3.1d). The daric weight of the Lampsakene gold staters and the fact that the silver tridrachms were equivalent in weight to double sigloi meant that this Greek coinage metrologically replicated the bimetallic Persian system.

Still under scholarly discussion, however, is the precise historical context of the coinage. Did Lysander conceive of this coinage when he took over the Spartan fleet in early 406/5 at Ephesos and ordered its implementation city by city as he sailed north from Rhodes to the Hellespont (Meadows 2011, 288n)? The coinage in that case would have been taken up in a sequence: Rhodes, Knidos, Iasos, and finally Lampsakos in the Hellespont before the battle at Aigospotamoi; minting would not have begun at Kyzikos, Byzantion, and Samos until he captured those cities after this final battle. It thus would have been inaugurated as a war coinage, adopted piecemeal as each city joined or was forced to join the alliance. But the coinage has an undeniably communal character and gives the impression rather of having been realized in a single deliberative act, which would belong most comfortably during Lysander's reorganization of the cities of the former Athenian empire beginning in 404 after Athens and finally Samos surrendered to him (Karwiese 1980). That reorganization would also link it to the start of a new era of anticipated unity under Spartan hegemony.

Furthermore, it would be aligned more closely with the Athenian imperial model in recognizing the desirability of a common currency for the collection of taxes or tribute, which the Spartans had begun to collect from the cities, and for the benefit of trade within the alliance. Although it resonates with what the Athenians had tried to achieve (with what success we don't know), the parallelism is inexact, in that this was a coinage organized by

Figure 7.11 Silver Chian-weight tridrachms = Persian-weight double sigloi of the "Alliance" (in Greek, *Synmachia*) under Sparta (*c*. 404–403 BC). The shared obverse type of all specimens shows the child Herakles strangling a snake with each hand and the legend Σ-Υ-Ν. Reverses are stamped with the badge and an abbreviated ethnic of the issuing city. (**a**) **Ephesos**: reverse showing a bee, Ε-Φ, and, below, the initial letters of the signing magistrate, Π-Ε, 11.12 g. *Paris*. (**b**) **Samos**: reverse with lion's scalp and the abbreviation Σ-Α, 11.29 g. *Leu (2001)*. (**c**) **Kyzikos**: reverse of lion's head above tunafish and KY-ZI. 11.41 g. *CNG (2016)*. (**d**) **Byzantion**: bull standing on a dolphin, with BY (using a local, pi-like form of B). 11.29 g. *Photograph © 2019 Museum of Fine Arts, Boston*. (**e**) **Iasos**: on the reverse, head of Apollo and [I]-A-Σ-I. 10.13 g. *ANS*. (**f**) **Knidos**: reverse head of Aphrodite with a ship's prow, and K-N-I. 10.89 g. *ANS*. (**g**) **Rhodes**: reverse type of rose with P-O. 10.86 g. *ANS*.

Figure 7.12 Gold daric of **Lampsakos** (*c.* 404–403 BC) with the same obverse image of young Herakles strangling snakes, and on the reverse the city emblem, the forepart of a winged horse. Uninscribed. 8.41 g. *Paris.*

Lysander but produced by his new allies themselves, arguably in a fiefdom separate from the Peloponnesian League.

The paucity of dies (for the major tridrachm denomination, one or two obverse dies per city, except for Ephesos, the Spartan headquarters in Ionia, with four obverse dies) and the rarity of fractions (at Kyzikos and Iasos only [Delrieux 2000, 194–6]) attest to the coinage's relatively short life, which corresponds to that of the brutal oligarchic regimes that Lysander set up in the cities. These were so oppressive and personally tied to Lysander that the authorities in Sparta had them removed and "decreed that the cities should be governed instead by their own ancestral laws" (Xen. *Hell.* 3.4.2). This marked the end of Lysander's alliance coinage, as the cities turned to minting coinages entirely of their own, yet virtually in every case on the now familiar Chian standard, which went on to become within a generation the nearly universal standard of coastal Asia Minor and its islands (Meadows 2011, 283–7).

8

Epilogue: From Tribute to Taxation

Kyzikos: City of Staters

And last of all, Kyzikos, the city full of staters

Yes, that reminds me of the time when I was on guard duty in the city

And I screwed a woman, a boy, and an old man for only a kollybos.
(Eupolis, *Poleis*, frag. 247)

Kyzikos is a fitting polis with which to conclude this book because its coinage and two extant lead weights provide unparalleled insights into one major subject city's relationship with Athens that we would not otherwise know about in such detail. Their coinage and the weights advertize, uniquely, as far as we know, a close relationship with Athens.

Kyzikos' electrum staters, the most important coinage in Black Sea and Propontine trade, were also one of the most significant in Aegean commerce generally. Kyzikos has even been termed "the second mint of the Athenian Empire" (Abramzon and Frolova 2007, 22), owing to its staters' acceptability in payments of tribute to Athens, their accumulation in the Treasury of Athena as a reserve coinage, and their release in some years, as noted in Chapter 3 (p. 43), in sizable amounts, for example, for financing a fleet in 418/7 off the Peloponnesian coast – during the Peace! Private individuals sought them as well for hoarding (recall the kyzikenes in Lysias' strongbox, p. 42).

In addition to their prominent economic roles in international commerce, in public and private savings, and in Athenian imperial finance, Kyzikene coins were minted with obverse types that were changed with each separate issue. And while most of these were traditional, generic types – like a sow (Fig. 3.1a) or other animals – some of the coin images carried unmistakeable political messages. This could not be clearer than in four fifth-century types that stand out for their unique references to Athenian mythology and ideology: the depictions of (1) Athens' first king, Kekrops, with his half-serpent, half-human body (Fig. 3.1d); (2) the birth of another legendary Athenian hero-king, Erechthonios, being raised up from the earth by his mother Ge (Fig. 3.1e); (3) the young Eleusinian hero Triptolemos riding in a flying chariot and bringing the gift of grain from Attica to all of humankind (*BMC* Mysia 63), and (4) the heroes in the charter myth of Athenian democracy, the "tyrannicides" Harmodios and Aristogeiton (Fig. 3.1c). All these coins are signed with the Kyzikene civic badge of a tunny fish below the main type.

To find these quintessentially Athenian figures showing up on the coinage of another state is nothing short of extraordinary. One wonders how widely such icons of Athenian culture were disseminated within the *arche*. But whatever the means of their transmission and the extent of their recognition elsewhere, these coin types of Kyzikos advertise a solidarity with Athens that could hardly be expressed more vividly. The types were probably chosen by the city mint officials responsible for the issue (p. 45), for there is no reason to think that the choice of these types came from an Athenian initiative.

This electrum coinage was not affected by the Coinage, Weights, and Measures Decree, which, as we have seen, was concerned exclusively with silver coinage. But although the Kyzikenes were free to mint and use their own electrum, they evidently would have had to use Athenian silver coinage as well. The weights used by the city for commercial purposes also needed to conform to the terms of the decree, which required that the weights be adjusted to the Athenian standard. The Kyzikenes went farther than that, however, in producing new weights that were boldly stamped with the unmistakable owl and olive sprig emblem of Athens towering over the small tunafish badge of Kyzikos and accompanied by a two-letter inscription that attests that this was a weight "of the city" (Fig. 6.6). The stamp demonstrates that the Kyzikenes had not only adopted the Attic metrological standard as their own but that, through the iconography (like that of the coinage), they chose to signal their alignment with the imperial city. We assume that these Attic-standard weights were probably produced in response to the mandate of the Athenian Decree on Coinages, Weights, and Measures, around 414 BC, although the possibility cannot be ruled out that Kyzikos, like the Elian officials for the Olympic Games of 420, might have adopted the weight standard of Athens voluntarily some years before (pp. 120–21).

Strategically located midway on the route between the Aegean and the Black Sea, Kyzikos mattered to Athens. From the lines of Eupolis' comedy quoted at the head of this chapter, we learn that Athens maintained an armed garrison there to ensure the city's loyalty and/or to protect the city from Persian pressure. (Kyzikos abutted the Persian satrapy of Phrygia and was the closest Greek city to the satrap's headquarters at Daskyleion.) But to appreciate Kyzikos' position as a strategic "partner" to Athens, we cannot do better than turn to its stamped economic instruments, coins and weights, that show how effective iconography could be as political expression. Let us now consider the *arche* at large to see how this linkage of the economic and political applies to the empire as a whole.

Transitioning to Empire-Wide Economic Uniformity

The Athenian empire has been viewed traditionally as a predominately political institution – for which the Coinage, Weights, and Measures Decree (or Decrees) has been regarded as the unequivocal exemplification. The influence of Moses Finley has been fundamental. Finley recognized the possibility that profit would come from reminting, and he noted that "the unprecedented volume of Athenian military and administrative payments, at a time when allied tribute was the largest source of public revenue, was much facilitated by a uniform coinage." But what immediately follows on this comment is critical for understanding his position. As he states, "Athens was now willing and able to demonstrate who was master within the empire by denying its subject-states the traditional symbol of autonomy, their own coins" (Finley 1973, 169).

Furthermore, seemingly to bolster the conviction that coinage was above all political, Finley claimed that minting by cities was a "nuisance," because the resulting variety of coinages compounded rather than facilitated problems of exchange – so therefore it must have been political (i.e., since it made no *economic* sense in his view). As he put it, "Given the political sense of coinage, it is not surprising that the autonomous Greek states made no substantial effort to abate the nuisance" (1973, 167). Missing from his assessment of the Decree, however, are weights and measures, which have no place in payments of tribute but are the foundation of trade and commercial taxes. In fact, as we argued in Chapter 6 (especially, p. 111), the convergence of uniform coinage, weights, and measures makes perfect sense when tied to the *eikoste*, which involved payments to Athens specifically when Athens decided to *abolish* tribute and impose custom taxes in the harbors of the *arche*.

Yet, in one respect, viewing the Coinage, Weights, and Measures Decree as political is absolutely correct, especially when one appreciates the perspective of Athens' subjects – a point that applies to every decree issued to these member states: any command from the imperial center was intended to force others to obey Athens' legal authority. Here is where the Coinage, Weights, and Measures Decree – and the *eikoste* – impinge directly on the autonomy of local taxation, which cities fiercely protected as their key source of revenue. Of course, Athenians, equally, will have recognized these decrees as political as well as economic, in that through them they were projecting their authority over members of the *arche*, while aiming at revenue and profit. Indeed, we need here to emphasize that the Coinage, Weights, and Measures Decree made rational, economic sense and must be viewed in that light, motivated as it was by an awareness that uniformity in commercial instruments would reduce the complexity of the new tax designed to bring in more revenue.

We have reviewed multiple examples of the Athenians' laissez faire attitude toward local minting. As long as there was a tributary system, the changes in local currency we surveyed in Chapter 3 were not due to political pressure. We noted that a reduction of allied minting, especially in large denominations, began already in the early decades of the *arche*. This decline is attributable, not to any legislation, but rather to the increased circulation of an almost unimaginable supply of coined silver from Laureion, the widespread availability and convenience of Athenian coinage in transactions, especially involving interstate commerce and military expenditures, and an understanding that it was the preferred currency for paying tribute and other obligations to Athens. For some allied cities this made continued minting of their own currency, or at least in large denominations, uneconomical.

But not all cities. We have seen (pp. 76–7) that Aegina continued to strike its stater-size coins after it was forced into the empire, which implies that Athens was not at that time mandating the exclusive use of its own coinage nor employing a prohibition of local coining as a punitive policy. Thasos and Samos, two islands that had revolted unsuccessfully, did experience an interval in minting upon their defeats, but then both resumed coining and did so in large denominations. From the Athenians' point of view, given the imposition of harsh demands such as indemnities for the cost of a siege, and then a substantial assessment of tribute, letting local minting (and commerce) continue, as a way of boosting the city's revenue base, was in their own interest.

Thasos provides an instructive case study. Upon resuming the minting of its staters, the island did so with a slight reduction in weight, which at 8.6 g made them equivalent to two Attic drachmas or half of a Euboean stater (p. 57, Fig. 3.13b). While, following its revolt, Thasos engaged in trade with its northern networks, it was also, for the first time, liable to pay tribute to Athens. Could it be that this shift to the Euboean-Attic standard is tied to their need to pay tribute? In any case there is no reason to think that this shift was an Athenian initiative.

When we turn to the coinage of Mytilene and the Troad following the suppression of the revolt of Mytilene and other cities on Lesbos (except Methymna) in 427 BC, the evidence is intriguing (pp. 95–8). While it is commonly assumed that Mytilene had to give up minting its renowned coinage of electrum *hektai*, it is unclear for how long. The changes in coinage that we do know about involve only smaller denominations among three entities: the Mytilenaians changed their billon coinage to drachmas and fractions in silver on the Attic weight system; three Aktaian cities freed from Mytilenaian control and brought into the Athenian *arche* minted parallel silver coinages; and those cities were followed by nearby cities which joined as partners in a regional trading network. As explained in Chapter 5, these monetary changes were evidently not the result of any direct imposition by Athens, but likely were local initiatives that began upon the transfer of the land on Lesbos to individual Athenians, who henceforth owned the land and received rents from the Lesbians.

The foregoing examples of non-interference contrast starkly with the insistence on uniformity in the Coinage, Weights, and Measures Decree. So what caused the radical changes comprising the legislation? It was, as we have proposed, the decision to raise more revenue from a new policy of universal taxation on trade. Implicitly, this led to a wholesale reconceptualizing of the *arche* as a single pan-Aegean economic entity that envisioned peace for the flourishing of commerce. Here it is worth recalling that tribute originated as the means by which the Delian League could carry on the annual military campaigns against Persia. By contrast, taxation on maritime commerce was specifically designed to fulfil the Athenians' need for revenue during peacetime, and for their expansionist aims. But while the *eikoste* with its need for uniform currency and commercial standards were conceived at a time of peace with Sparta, war resumed shortly, when the Athenians most glaringly broke the Peace by joining an Argive campaign in Peloponnesian territory (summer of 414, Thuc. 6.105). This leaves us to guess what might have been. Any perception that the Peace of Nikias would endure instantly evaporated not only by that campaign but also by the dispatch of a Peloponnesian army to Sicily to aid Syracuse, and the permanent fortification of Dekeleia shortly after. We're left with tantalizing tidbits: the *eikostologos* at Aegina virtually at the end of the war, and

Thrasyboulos' campaigns to collect the tax at Klazomenai and at Thasos in the late 390s.

The Empire in Broader Context: Looking Around and Forward

Still, we should like to put these monetary and metrological decisions in a wider context. Were the Athenians envisioning uniform standards across the *arche* as a way – from their perspective – to promote economic stability, unity, and peace (and adherence to them as rulers)? Uniformity of coinage and standards is a pronounced feature of nations, empires, and federations that want to project, and reinforce, concord and stability, from the first Chinese empire of the third century BC (the Qin, with inscriptions on weights attesting to the peace and stability of the realm [Pines 2014]), and the Hellenistic Leagues, to the Roman empire, all the way up to the European monetary Union. Some of these comparanda tie their economic measures and purpose to an ideology supporting the ruling center; thus, they promote a practical vision of their empires through harmony and prosperity through the adoption of uniformity. These examples are suggestive because they are aligned with the behavior and the principles that we can discern operating in the Athenian *arche*, though implicitly more than explicitly.

We have emphasized the economically rational foundation for the twin measures – the *eikoste,* and with it, the Coinage, Weights, and Measures Decree – and the pronounced change away from the empire's tributary structure: instead of delineating "ruler and subject," the Athenians were advertising their imperial relations in terms of hegemon and "allies" (*symmachoi*). Nevertheless, it is vital to recognize that the goal remained the same. That was precisely the extraction of monetary resources from the empire in order to increase profits at the expense of other Greeks.

Guide to Further Reading

An excellent concise guide to methods and approaches in numismatics from a historical perspective is C. Howgego's *Ancient History from Coins* (1995). The standard survey for classical Greek coins is still C. Kraay's *Archaic and Classical Greek Coins* (1976), reliable except where it employs the Coinage, Weights, and Measures Decree as a chronological anchor. *The Oxford Handbook of Greek and Roman Coinage*, ed. W. E. Metcalf (2012), contains valuable chapters that illuminate not only coins of the Greek cities but also Persian coinage. When we move to historical studies of the empire and coinage, see M. Trundle, "Coinage and the Economics of the Athenian Empire," in J. A. Armstrong, ed., *Circum Mare: Themes in Ancient Warfare* (2016); and Howgego, "Why Did the Ancients Strike Coins?" (1990). Full references in Bibliography.

The writings of T. Rihll (2001) and P. Christensen (2005), cited also in the Bibliography provide authoritative accounts of the industrial processing of the lead-silver ore at Laureion; and P. van Alfen has written on the administration of Athenian minting policies in "Hatching Owls: The Regulation of Coin Production in Later Fifth-Century Athens," in F. de Callataÿ, ed., "Quantifying Monetary Supplies in Greco-Roman Times," *Pragmateiai* 19 (2011): 127–49.

For a concise survey of the period, see P. J. Rhodes, *A History of the Classical Greek World*, 2nd ed. (2005). R Meiggs's *The Athenian Empire* (1972) is foundational for its comprehensive treatment of the empire, but its narrow political perspective and its chronology have been overtaken by more recent scholarship that gives ample attention to the empire's economic context. M. I. Finley, "The Fifth Century Athenian Empire: A Balance Sheet," in P. D. A. Garnsey and C. R. Whittaker, *Imperialism in the Ancient World* (1978) is an important analysis of the various means by which Athens extracted revenue from the empire. A useful collection of sources for the empire, with commentary, can be found in R. Osborne, ed. and trans., *The Athenian Empire*, Lactor 1, 4th ed. (2007). For a valuable discussion of the epigraphic sources for the empire, see P. J. Rhodes, "After the Three-Bar Sigma Controversy: The History of Athenian Imperialism Reassessed," *Classical Quarterly* (2008) 58: 500–6.

For discussion of economies, both in Athens and the cities of the empire: A. Bresson (English translation by S. Rendall), *The Making of the Ancient Greek Economy: Institutions, Markets and Growth in the City-States* (2016); L. Nixon and S. Price, "The Size and Resources of Greek Cities," in O. Murray and S. Price, eds., *The Greek City from Homer to Alexander* (1990): 137–70; D. M. Pritchard, *Public Spending and Democracy in Classical Athens* (2015). J. Ma, N. Papazarkadas, and R. Parker, eds., *Interpreting the Athenian Empire* (2009) contains a number of wide-ranging chapters; see also L. Kallet, "The Origins of the Athenian Economic *Arche," Journal of Hellenic Studies* 133 (2013):49–60; E. Bissa, *Governmental Intervention in Foreign Trade in Archaic and Classical Greece* (2009).

L. J. Samons II, ed., *Cambridge Companion to the Age of Pericles* (2007), contains a number of highly readable and valuable chapters, especially those that focus on democracy, empire, institutions and finance. So too, the chapters in R. Osborne and S. Hornblower, eds., *Ritual, Finance and Politics: Democratic Accounts Presented to David Lewis* (1994). Also the chapters in P. Low, ed., *The Athenian Empire* (2008), with an unsurpased bibliography.

Appendix A Weight Standards and Denominational Systems

1. Coin Weights

The great variation in the standard weight units and denominational divisions of Greek coinages in Archaic and Classical Greece is the product of centuries of local borrowing and adaptation of various older metrological traditions, including the weight systems of the ancient Near East and, during the Early Iron Age, the use of iron spits as a means of valuation in the Peloponnesos.

A. In the fifth century BC, most of the standard coin units were employed with a denominational structure that was based on a *stater* or standard coin unit that was sometimes divided into halves, and almost always into *hektai* or sixths, often with further subdivisions of twelfths, twenty-fourths, and, rarely, forty-eighths. In the Athenian empire, five weight standards employed this system:

> *Euboean* standard: stater of 17.2 g and *hekte* of 2.86 g.
>
> *Phokaian* standard (used, probably exclusively, for electrum coinages): stater of 16.1 g and *hekte* of 2.68 g.
>
> *Chian* standard: ideal stater of 15.6 g. The staters of 7.8 g coined during most of the fifth century were actually half-staters and the thirds of 2.6 g were actually sixths. A (quarter stater or) drachma of 3.9 g was introduced *c.* 410 BC, at which time the Chians also began to mint (tetradrachm) staters of full, 15.6 g weight.
>
> *Milesian* standard: stater of 14.2 g, and *hekte* of 2.4 g. In the fifth century sometimes divided also into fourths or drachmas (3.55 g).
>
> *Parian-Thasian* standard (of coastal Thrace): stater of *c.* 10 g. Possibly a reduced version of the Aeginetan standard (Psoma 2015, 175–9).

B. Silver coins of Aegina and of other cities that adopted the *Aeginetan Standard* employed a stater of 12.4 g with the same divisional structure as earlier, but the twelfths (= 1.0 g) were called obols (literally and originally meaning iron "spits"). Six of these silver obols made up a half-stater (6.2 g), which was called a drachma (literally "a handful," that is, of spits).

C. The *Attic Standard* and denominational structure was a hybrid system. The dominant unit was the tetradrachm, which had the same weight as the 17.2 g stater of the Euboeic standard, but was divided into four drachmas of 4.3 g, each of which was divided (like Aeginetan drachmas) into six obols (0.72 g). In the fifth century Athens minted also half-obols and, infrequently, quarter-obols (0.36 and 0.18 g).

D. The silver coinage of Samos employed the Athenian divisions of drachmas and obols but on the *Samian* standard of a lighter 13.1 g tetradrachm.

E. Silver "drachmas" and "didrachmas" minted by some Greek cities of or very close to Asia Minor (e.g., in the Hellespontine region, Kolophon, Phaselis) on the *Persian* standard were adjusted to the weight of a Persian silver siglos (5.5 g) or double siglos (*c.* 11 g).

F. In a recent review of some archaic and fifth-century coinages in the regions of the Hellespont and Troad, Ellis-Evans and van Alfen (2018) propose the existence of a local "Troad" standard, with a stater of 15.4 g (electrum of Lampsakos) and smaller divisions in silver, beginning with a *c.* 3.8 g drachma.

G. Many civic coinages, especially but by no means exclusively in small denominations, were intentionally minted slightly underweight as a means of conserving silver and to realize a profit when full-weight foreign coins had to be exchanged for them on a 1:1 basis in order to do business in the city (Konuk 1998, 200; Psoma 2013, 57–61). The weights of the Aeginetic-standard staters of Kaunos and Teos are about 4 percent or one Aeginetic half-obol (0.5 g) below full weight. Accordingly, the staters of Ainos (Fig. 3.17a) and Kos (Fig. 3.27b), sometimes identified as triple sigloi, might actually be reduced Euboean staters or reduced Attic tetradrachms since they were about 4 percent or one Attic obol (0.7 g) below standard. Triple sigloi were, however, briefly minted at Rhodes around 408–404 BC (Ashton 2001, 80, 99), when Rhodes was allied with Sparta and was also minting double sigloi (Fig. 7.11e).

H. Large monetary sums in all Greek coinages were expressed in two weight units of account: the mina (*mna*) and the talent. At Athens the mina was made up of 100 drachmas (435 g) and the talent consisted of 60 minas, i.e., 6,000 drachmas (26.1 kg).

2. The Athenian Trade Weight Standard

Greek cities, whether or not they minted a precious metal coinage, employed a comprehensive weight standard and system for the routine measuring of all commodities and items other than coins: agricultural products, base metals, textiles, other manufactured goods, and so on. In some cities and regions (for example, where Aeginetan- or Euboean- weight coinage was used), the standard of the coin weight and the standard of the trade weight were normally the same; in other places the two weight systems diverged. As known from inscribed balance weights from Athens (Kroll 2020), before *c.* 500 BC the city had a unified weight system: the monetary mina of 100 Athenian silver drachmas (435 g) was equal in mass to the trade mina. However, probably around 480 BC, the Athenians raised their trade weight standard by 5 percent, making the weight of the trade mina equivalent to 105 silver drachmas (457 g). By the end of the fifth century (Andok. 1.83) and in the late fourth-century BC Aristotelian *Constitution of Athens* (10.2), this 105-drachma mina was attributed to the early Athenian lawgiver Solon. While this attribution to Solon was wildly anachronistic, it reveals how fundamentally "Athenian" this highly anomalous trade standard had come to be regarded. It was, after all, the trade standard of Athens during its fifth-century *arche* and was the trade standard that Athens increasingly propagated throughout the *arche* (pp. 119–21).

Since there is evidence that the Athenians valued their own silver coinage as being worth more than unminted silver and non-Athenian silver coins by probably a difference of 5 percent (pp. 115–16), some numismatists have speculated that the heavier trade mina (which was 5 percent heavier than the coin mina) was created to faciliate exchange between Athenian coinage and all other silver (Mørkholm 1982, 291–2; Le Rider 2001, 256–60), in particular when massive quantities of such silver might have been submitted in tribute after 478 (Konuk 2011, 63n). Alongside their coin mina of 100 silver drachmas, if the Athenians used a second mina with a mass of 105 drachmas for weighing everything else, including bags of bullion or of non-Athenian silver coins, upon weighing they would know in an instant that each mina of silver in the bags was exactly equivalent in value to a mina of Athenian silver coinage.

However, late fifth-century inventories of dedications on the Athenian Acropolis reveal that some precious metal objects, like the Nikai in the Parthenon, each of which was made of two 6,000-drachma talents of gold (Thompson 1970), were weighed not by the trade mina (which would have given a trade talent of 6,300 drachmas) but by the 100-drachma coin mina, implying that the latter was, in fact, used by the Athenians for weighing at least their own unminted gold. Another suggestion is that the trade mina was raised, perhaps, for the more accurate measuring of grain, the most abundant and essential commodity in Greek commerce (Van Wees 2013, 119).

But in the most recent study of early fifth-century Athenian bronze weights (Kroll 2020, 58–61, 67–8), the earliest weight on the 105 standard is shown to have been converted in haste from a slightly older weight on the 100-drachma standard, most likely in 480 as the Athenians were preparing to abandon the city to the invading Persians prior to the Battle of Salamis. If correct, this means that the increase in weight was probably authorized as an emergency measure to reduce the cost of food and other essential commodities at this time of crisis.

Appendix B   Hoards

Coins are of silver, unless specified otherwise.

A. **Hoards recovered within the territory of the Athenian** *arche*, **478–404 BC** (excluding hoards that are unreliably reported)

Single-Mint Hoards
Attica

1. **Athens Acropolis, 480–478 BC.** Sixty-two late archaic Athenian coins: tetradrachms from the last of the "unwreathed" Owl series and earlier fractions. Excavated from the Persian destruction debris of 480.
   IGCH 13 (Athens, Acropolis 1886)
2. **Sounion, *c.* 480–470 BC.** Three Athenian tetradrachms, one didrachm, one drachm. "Probably incomplete."
   IGCH 14 (Sounion c. 1936)
3. **Attica, *c.* 470–465 BC.** Eight Early Classical Athenian tetradrachms, one drachma.
   IGCH 16 (Attica, before 1906)
4. **Piraeus, late to end of fifth century BC.** Twenty-nine Athenian coins of late standardized type (tetradrachms, drachmas). Pot hoard from excavations. See p. 24.
   CH 5. 14 (Piraeus 1977)
5. **Ano Voula, late to end of fifth century BC.** Thirty Athenian coins of late standardized type (tetradrachms, drachmas, one triobol). Pot hoard in excavation, north of Piraeus, overlooking the coast at ancient Halai Aixonides (Map 2.1). See p. 24.
   CH 10. 15 (Ano Voula 1979)
5a. **Piraeus, 406–404 BC.** "Thousands" of silver-plated bronze drachmas and tetradrachms. See p. 134, Fig. 7.9.
   IGCH 46 (1902); Kroll 1996.

Islands

6. **Eretria, Euboea, 440s (447?) BC.** 138 Athenian coins mostly of Early-standardized tetradrachms, and drachmas, together with 2 older Eretrian didrachms. Pot hoard in excavations in the city agora. Probably dating to the attempted revolt of 447. See pp. 48–9, 70.
   CH 8. 69 and CH 9.17 (Eretria 1981); Flament 2007a, 62.

7. **Eretria, Euboea, last quarter fifth century BC.** Forty Athenian coins (tetradrachms, drachmas, and triobols). Found in excavations near the agora. Probably dating to the revolt of 411. See pp. 48–9, 70.
   CH 9.11 (Eretria 1976)

8. **Euboea, later fifth century BC.** Sixty-seven Athenian tetradrachms in a pot (probably at Eretria). See pp. 48–9, 70.
   IGCH 39 (Euboea 1921)

9. **Paros, *c.* 465 BC.** *c.* 100 Parian drachmas.
   IGCH 13 (Paros 1936). Kagan 2008, 108.

10. **Paros, *c.* 470 BC.** *c.* 600 Aeginetan staters.
    CH 2. 24 (Eirene, Paros)

11. **Kythnos, *c.* 460 BC.** Thirty-one fractions of Kythnos.
    CH 9. 15 (Kythnos 1976)

12. **Aegina, *c.* 450 BC(?).** Seven obols of Aegina, one triobol of Phocis.
    CH 3. 9 (Angistri, Aegina, 1975)

Thraceward

13. **Mende, *c.* 423 BC.** *c.* 200 staters of Mende, one of Akanthos.
    IGCH 358 (Kaliandra/Mende 1913); Kagan 2014, 5–11.

14. **Akanthos, *c.* 480–460 BC.** 150+ staters and fractions of Akanthos.
    IGCH 357 (Hierissos/ Akanthos 1934)

15. **Akanthos, *c.* 450 BC(?).** Four *hektai* of Akanthos in tomb.
    CH 6. 9 (Hierissos/Akanthos)

16. **Abdera, *c.* 450 BC (?).** Thirteen+ staters of Abdera.
    IGCH 698 (Abdera c. 1850)

17. **Samothrace, *c.* 460 BC.** *c.* 100 coins of Samothrace: 1 didrachm stater; the rest hemidrachms and smaller fractions.
    IGCH 696 (Kiourpet, Samothrace, 1930); Gérin 2009.

Hellespontine

18. **Bisanthe, 480–450 BC**. Sixty-six+ drachmas of Parion. See p. 7.
    IGCH 697 (Tekirdag, Thrace, 1957)
19. **Kios, fifth century BC**. Thirty silver "obols" of Kyzikos. See p. 7.
    CH 4. 14 (Gemlik, Bursa, Turkey, 1972)
20. **Lesbos, mid-fifth century BC**. Fifty-six+ coins (staters, thirds and sixths) of Methymna.
    IGCH 1187 (Lesbos before 1892)

Ionia

21. **Chios (?), c. 489–475 BC**. Twenty-four staters of Chios.
    CH 7. 14 (Chios 1980)
22. **Chios, c. 425 BC**. Fifty-nine coins (staters and thirds) of Chios in pot found in excavations.
    IGCH 1191 (Phanai on Chios 1913); Hardwick 2010, 240.
23. **Chios (?), c. 420 BC**. Twenty-six+ staters of Chios.
    IGCH 1179 (Chios? c. 1933); Hardwick 2010, 240.
24. **Ionia, fifth century BC**. Twenty-one obols of Miletos, one obol of Ialysos.
    IGCH 1195 (Ionia before 1940)

Karia

25. **Bodrum (ancient Halikarnassos), Turkey, mid-fifth century BC**. *c.* 2,000 drachmas of Knidos.
    IGCH 1186 (Bodrum 1875)
26. **Karia?, last quarter, fifth century BC** *c.* 100 drachmas of Knidos.
    IGCH 1193 (Caria? c. 1966)

Mixed Hoards

Thraceward

27. **Skione, c. 423 BC**. Forty-five staters of Skione, ninety+ of Mende, seventy of Akanthos.
    CH VII.63 (Skione 1991); CH IX.4; Kagan 2014, 7–11.

28. **Olynthos excavations, late 420s BC.** Twelve *hekai* of Akanthos, three of Chalcidian League, three of Perdikkas II; one drachma of Athens. See p. 35.

    IGCH 359 (Olynthos 1931); Kagan 2014: 13n.

29. **Chalkidike, *c.* 420 BC.** Sixteen+ fractions from Chalkidian League, Mende, Skione, Terone, Dikaia, and Thasos.

    CH I.18 (Chalkidike 1962); Psoma 2001, 152–153; Kagan 2014, 10n.

30. **Chalkidike, late fifth century BC.** 1,220+ *hektai*: 464+ of Akanthos, 40+ Olynthos, 300+ of Chalkidian League, 300 Perdikas II, 70+ Terone, 1 Mende. All dispersed.

    CH 9. 15 (Macedonia 1994)

31. **Poteidaia, end of fifth century BC.** Fifty-four+ fractions: thirty-eight (including one bronze coin) from Mende, one to a few from King Archelaos of Macedonia, Akanthos, Aineia, Poteidaia, Skione, Orchomenos, Thebes, other Boeotia.

    IGCH 360 (Nea Cassandra c. 1897); Psoma 2001, 153–154.

Ionia

32. **Ionia, mid-fifth century BC.** Six quarter-obols of Kolophon, stater and two fractions of Teos.

    IGCH 1190 (Western Asia Minor c. 1936)

33. **Ionia, *c.* 450 BC.** Fractions of Athens (1), Klazomenai? (2), Kolophon (5), Magnesia? (2), Teos (1).

    IGCH 1189 (Western Asia Minor, c. 1930)

34. **Ionia, *c.* 400 BC.** 216+ fractions (diobols and below) of Miletus, Teos, and Kebren.

    CH 8. 72 (Ionia, 1989)

35. **Klazomenai, *c.* 410–400 BC.** Seventy electrum staters of Kyzikos, twenty electrum staters of Lampsakos. Several Persian gold darics. See p. 130.

    IGCH 1194 (Vourla? 1875)

36. **Erythrai mid-fifth century BC.** *C.* seventy-nine+ Electrum hektai of Mytilene and Phocaea, with sixteen+ silver coins ("didrachms" of Klazomenai, Erythrai and "drachmas" of Chios).

    IGCH 1184 (Erythrae c. 1923)

B. **Hoards recovered outside of the Athenian *arche* containing a significant component of Athenian Owl tetradrachms, 480s–early fourth century BC.**

37. **Methone (Macedonia), mid-fifth century BC.** Found in 2006 excavations in two lots; one of nine noticeably worn staters of Alexander I of Macedon (died *c.* 453 BC); the other of twelve Early Standardized Athenian tetradrachms. Methone did not become an ally of Athens until 431. See p. 70.

    Ch. Gazolis and S. Psoma, publication in preparation.

38. **Gela (Sicily), *c.* 485.** 187 Archaic Owls, among *c.* 1,076 coins from seven mints.

    IGCH 2066 (Gela 1956)

39. **Naxos (Sicily), 403 BC.** Twenty-two tetradrachms: seventeen of Sicilian cities, five late Standardized Owls of Athens, all in a small clay vessel, excavated from a destroyed apartment building. See p. 24.

    Flament 2007a, 219–220, pls. 24.3, 24.12, 25.7, 27.4.

40. **Asyut (Egypt), 475–470 BC.** 127 Archaic Owls, among 681+ coins from sixty-seven mints.

    IGCH 1644 (Asyut, 1968 or 1969)

41. **Elmalı (Lycia), *c.* 460 BC.** 161 Owl tetradrachms and 13 decadrachms, among 1,900 coins from more than thirty mints. See pp. 9–11, 67, 78.

    CH 8. 48 (Elmalı, Lycia, Turkey, 1984).

42. **Malayer (Western Iran), *c.* 440 BC.** 163 Owls and cut fragments, among *c.* 375 coins from twenty-eight, predominately Greek, mints. See pp. 20, 26.

    IGCH 1790 (Malayer, c. 1934); Meadows, in preparation.

43. **Jordan, *c.* 440s BC.** 10 Owls and 20 cut fragments (including one of a decadrachm), among 113 coins from about thirty mints, plus ingots, and jewelry.

    IGCH 1482 (Jordan, Houran region 1967)

44. **Carchemish (North Syria), *c.* 440 BC.** 312 Owl tetradrachms and 3 decadrachms, among c. 400 coins including 39 Bisalti tristaters (9 with, 30 without inscriptions) and 5 of Alexander I (inscribed reverse). Dispersed. See pp. 10, 79.

    (1994. Publication in preparation by A. Meadows and U. Wartenberg)

45. **Southeast Asia Minor, c. 430s or 420s BC.** 16,000 Owls among 24,000 coins. Most of the non-Athenian silver comes from local mints of Cyprus and cities along the Asia Minor coast. Possibly assembled for Persian military or naval pay. Dispersed. See p. 45.

    (2017. Information from multiple sources)

46. **Zagazig (Egypt), late sixth to early fourth century BC.** Thirty-four Owls (eighteen post–480 to early fourth century BC), among eighty-four archaic coins from about twenty-five mints and eighteen ingots. See pp. 7–8, Fig. 1.3.

    IGCH 1648 (Zagazig, Egypt 1901)

47. **Tell el-Maskhouta, (Egypt), early fourth century BC.** 6,000+ Owls. See p. 35.

    IGCH 1649 (Tell el-Maskhouta 1947–1948)

48. **Fayum (Egypt), early fourth century BC.** 347 Owls.

    CH 10. 442 (Fayum 1943–1944); Arnold-Biucchi 2006-07.

49. **North Syria, c. 400 BC.** Reported total of 10,000 Owls, recovered in 2007 near Aleppo. See p. 35.

    Buxton 2009

50. **Turkey, c. 400 BC.** Said to include 1,300 Owls and two staters of Akanthos, recovered in 1980s. Dispersed. A portion illustrated in Fig. 2.10. See p. 35.

    Kroll 2009, fig. 8.1; Konuk 2011, 60.

51–55. **South Central and Eastern Asia Minor, c. 400/early fourth century BC. Lycaonia:** *IGCH 1243* (70+ Owls, 1 Persian adaptation [Fig. 2.11]); **Cilicia:** *IGCH 1255* (c. 200 Owls), *IGCH 1259* (35 Owls), *CH 5.15* (300 Owls), *CH 9. 390* (127 Owls).

Appendix C Glossary of Numismatic Terms

Authority
The formal guarantor of the value of a coin. For civic coinages, the authority was generally the government of the city itself. Within kingdoms and empires, the authority was usually the supreme ruler (e.g., king, emperor) or an appointee (e.g., satrap or provincial governor).

Billon
An alloy of silver heavily debased with copper.

Circulation
The movement of coinage once it has been issued.

Control–mark
A symbol, usually on the reverse of a coin, indicating some aspect of the administration of coin production.

Denomination
The value of an ancient coin. These values are generally expressed in a standard set of units, subdivisions, and multiples. See Appendix A.

Die
A piece of metal engraved with a design in sunken relief and then used strike coins. Two dies were required to strike the two faces of a coin: the **obverse die** and the **reverse die**.

Die-engraver
The artist responsible for the engraving of the design on to the dies. The engravers are generally anonymous on ancient coinage, although a few signatures are recorded, particularly in late fifth-century Sicily.

Die study
A technical numismatic study of a coinage that involves the identification of the dies used to strike a coinage. Such studies allow for the establishment of the relative chronology of a coinage. They also permit quantification of a coinage by identifying the number of dies used to produce a given coinage.

Electrum
An alloy of gold and silver. Although it occurs naturally in various proportions of the two components, when used in ancient coinage it was almost always in a carefully controlled artificial mixture.

Emergency hoard
A hoard of coins and perhaps other precious objects secreted together in antiquity at a time of emergency.

	Such deposits tend to consist of a cross-section of coins in **circulation** at the time of deposit.
Ethnic	A **legend** indicating the collective group of people (usually the citizens of a city) acting as the authority behind a coinage.
Fiduciary	Coinage that takes it value not from the character and quantity of the metal it contains, but from the *fiat* of the authority behind it.
Flan	The metal blank from which a coin is struck.
Hoard	A group of coins deposited together in antiquity, and thus forming a single archaeological context for multiple objects. The reasons for deposit are varied, and they are rarely recoverable with certainty from the deposits themselves. The two main categories are **savings hoards** and **emergency hoards**.
Imitation	A coin that, more or less slavishly, copies the types of a model coinage but is not a product of the same **authority** as its model.
Intrinsic	A coin that takes it value from the character and quantity (weight) of metal that it contains.
Issue	Either the process of officially placing a coin into circulation; or a specific subsection or phase of coin production, identifiable by a specific control mark or mint magistrate's signature.
Legend	The inscription(s) that appear on a coin, most commonly found on the reverse.
Mint	A place where coins are produced.
Mint-magistrates	The officials, whether elected or appointed, responsible for oversight of the production of coins within the mint. The names of most private individuals that appear on Greek coins are assumed to be those of mint-magistrates. In democratic Athens the position was staffed by an annual board of ten supervisors.
Monogram	An identifying mark made up of a number of letters, usually of the initial letters of the name of a mint-magistrate.
Obverse	The "heads" side of a coin, produced by the obverse (or lower) die. See Fig. 1.4.

Reverse	The "tails" side of the coin, produced by the reverse (or upper) die. See Fig. 1.4.
Savings hoard	A group of coins gathered together in a single deposit over a period of time, for the purpose of saving.
Strike	The process by which Greek coins were produced. It consists of placing a blank (flan) of metal on the **obverse die**, positioning the **reverse die** on top of the blank, and then applying force in the form of hammer blows (striking) to imprint the designs of the two dies on to the piece of metal. See Fig. 1.4.
Test-cut	A cut made into an **intrinsic** value coin to ensure that it is made of solid metal, and not plated.
Type	The numismatic term for the design that appears on a coin; this may thus be subdivided into **obverse** and **reverse** types.
Weight-standard	The official system of weights in use in an ancient state. See Appendix A.

Bibliography

Translations

Herodotus, The Histories. Translation by R. Waterfield. Oxford World's Classics. Oxford, 1998.

The Landmark Xenophon's Hellenika. Translation by J. Marincola. New York, 2009.

Thucydides, The Peloponnesian War. Translation by M. Hammond. Oxford World's Classics. Oxford, 2009.

References

Abramzon, M. C., and Frolova, N. A. 2007. "Le trésor de Myrmekion de statères cyzicenes." *Revue Numismatique* 163: 15–44.

Agut-Labordère, D. 2016. "De l'amidonnier contre de l'orge: le sens de la conversion des quantités dans les ostraca démotiques de 'Ayn Manâwir (Oasis de Kharga, Égypte)." *Comptabilités* 8: 2–8.

Alram, M. 2012. "The coinage of the Persian empire." In *The Oxford Handbook of Greek and Roman Coinage*, ed. W. E. Metcalf. Oxford: 61–87.

Aperghis, G. 1997–98. "A reassessment of the Laurion mining lease records." *Bulletin of the Institute of Classical Studies* 42: 1–20.

    2013. "Athenian mines, coins and triremes." *Historia* 62: 1–24.

Archibald, Z. A. 2013. *Ancient Economies of the Northern Aegean, Fifth to First Centuries BC*. Oxford.

Arnold-Biucchi, C. 2006–07. "La trouvaille de Fayoum 1933–1934 et le problem des chouettres égyptiennes." *Annuaire de l'École pratique des hautes études, Section des sciences historiques et philologiques. Résumés des conferences et travaux* 139: 91.

Ashton, R. H. J. 2001. "The coinage of Rhodes 408–c.190 BC." In *Money and Its Uses in the Ancient Greek World*, eds. A. Meadows and K. Shipton. Oxford: 79–115.

Ashton, R., and Hurter, S., eds. 1998. *Studies in Greek Numismatics in Memory of Martin Jessop Price*. London.

Barron, J. P. 1966. *The Silver Coins of Samos*. London.

    1968. "The fifth-century diskoboloi of Kos." In *Studies in Greek Coinage Presented to Stanley Robinson*, eds. C. M. Kraay and J. G. Jenkins. Oxford: 78–89.

Blomberg, P. 1996. *On Corinthian Iconography: The Bridled Winged Horse and the Helmeted Female Head in the Sixth Century BC*. Stockholm.

Brackmann, S. 2015. "Alexandros I. oder Bisaltai." *Jahrbuch für Numismatik und Geldgeschichte* 65: 1–8.

Bresson, A. 2016. "Revue article" of Grandjean and A. Moustaka (eds.) 2013. *American Journal of Numismatics* 28: 259–71.

Brousseau, L. 2013. "La naissance de la monnaie de bronze en Grande Grece et en Sicile." In Grandjean and Moustaka (eds.), 81–96.

Buttrey, T. V. 1982. "Pharonic imitations of Athenian tetradrachms." In *Proceedings of the 9th International Congress of Numismatic Studies, Berne, September 1979*, ed. T. Hackens and R. Weiler. Louvain-La Neuve-Luxembourg: 137–40.

Buxton, R. F. 2009. "The Northern Syria 2007 hoard of Athenian owls: behavioral aspects." *American Journal of Numismatics* 21: 1–27.

Callataÿ, F. de. 2011. "Quantifying monetary production in Greco-Roman times: a general frame." In *Quantifying Monetary Supplies in Graeco-Roman Times* (Pragmateiai 19), ed. F. de Callataÿ. Bari: 7–29.

Canevaro, M., and Rutter, K. 2014. "Silver for Syracuse: the Athenian defeat and the period of the 'signing artists.'" *Schweizerische Numismatische Rundschau* 93: 5–20.

Carradice, I., ed. 1987. *Coinage and Administration in the Athenian and Persian Empires. The 9th Oxford Symposium on Coinage and Monetary History*. Oxford.
   1987. "The 'regal' coinage of the Persian empire.'" In Carradice (ed.), 73–93.

Christensen, P. 2005. "Economic rationalism in fourth-century BCE Athens." *Greece and Rome* 50: 31–56.

Conophagos, C. 1980. *Le Laurium antique et la technique grecque de la production de l'argent*. Athens.

Coupar, S.-A. 2000. *The Chronology and Development of the Coinage of Corinth to the Peloponnesian War*. PhD thesis, University of Glasgow.

Davis, G. 2014. "Mining money in late archaic Athens." *Historia* 63: 257–77.

Davis, G., and Sheedy, K. 2019. "Miltiades II and his alleged minting in the Chersonesos." *Historia* 68: 11–24.

Delrieux, F. 2000. "Les ententes monétaires au type et à la legend ΣYN au debut du IVe siècle." In *Méchanismes et innovations monétaires dans l'Anatolie achéménide: actes de la table ronde internationale d'Istanbul, 22–23 mai 1977*, ed. O. Casabonne. Paris: 185–211.

Ellis-Evans, A. 2016. "Mytilene, Lampsakos, Chios and the financing of the Spartan fleet (406–404)." *Numismatic Chronicle* 176: 1–19.
   2018. *The Kingdom of Priam, Lesbos and the Troad between Anatolia and the Aegean*. Oxford.

Ellis-Evans, A., and Kagan, J. In preparation. Expanded version of "Imperialism and regionalism in the Athenian empire: an Attic weight coinage from north-west Turkey and its aftermath (427–405 BC)." http://numismatics.org/pocketch ange/ellis-evans/
   forthcoming."Bimetallism, coinage, and empire in Persian Anatolia." Revision of paper presented at the conference, Coinage in Imperial Space, Krakow, June 28–July 2, 2017. www.coinageinimperialspace.org/Speakers-Abstracts/

Ellis-Evans, A., and Van Alfen, P. 2018. "Preliminary observations on the archaic silver coinage of Lampsakos in its regional context." In Tekin (ed.), 41–52.

Erol-Özdizbay, A. 2018. "The coinage of Pordosilene (Pordoselene/Poroselene)." In Tekin (ed.), 66–83.

Faucher, T., Marcellesi, M.-C., and Picard, O., eds. 2011. *Nomisma: La circulation monétaire dans la monde grec antique*, Acts du colloque international, Athens 14–17 avril 2010. Athens.

Fawcett, P. 2016. "When I squeeze you with eisphorai": Taxes and tax policy in Classical Athens," *Hesperia* 85: 153–99.

Figueira, T. J. 1998. *The Power of Money: Coinage and Politics in the Athenian Empire*. Philadelphia.

Finley, M. I. 1973. *The Ancient Economy*. 2nd ed. Berkeley.

Fischer-Bossert, W. 2008. *The Athenian Decadrachm*. New York.

Flament, C. 2007a. *Le monnayage en argent d'Athènes de l'époque archaïque à l'époque hellénistique (c. 550–c. 40 av. J.-C.)*. Louvain-la-Neuve.

2007b. *Une économie monétarisée: Athènes à l'époque classique (440-338); Contribution à l'étude du phénomène monétaire en Grèce ancienne*. Louvain.

2007c. "L'atelier Athénien: réflexions sur la politique monétaire d'Athènes à l'époque classique." In *Liber amicorum Tony Hackens*, ed. G. Moucharte et al. Louvain-la-Neuve: 1–10.

2011. "Retour sur les critères qui défissent habituellement les 'imitations' Athèniennes." In *Proceedings of The XIV International Numismatic Congress, Glasgow 2009*, ed. N. Holmes. Glasgow: 170–7.

Flament, C., Lateano, O., and Demortier, G. 2008. "Quantitative analysis of Athenian coinage by PIXE." In *Proceedings of the 4th Symposium of the Hellenic Society of Archaeometry, National Hellenic Research Foundation, Athens, 28-31 May 2003*, ed. Y. Facorellis et al. (BAR International Series 1746). Oxford: 445–50.

Fried, S. 1987. "The decadrachm hoard: an introduction." In Carradice (ed.), 1–10.

Gabrielsen, V. 2013. "Finance and taxes." In *A Companion to Ancient Greek Government*, ed. H. Beck. Oxford: 332–48.

Gale, N. H., Genter, W., and Wagner, G. A. 1980. "Mineralogical and geographical silver sources of archaic Greek coinage." In *Metallurgy in Numismatics, Royal Numismatic Society Special Publication No. 13*, ed. D. M. Metcalf. London: 3–50.

Gatzolis, C. 2013. "New evidence on the beginning of bronze coinage in northern Greece." In Grandjean and Moustaka (eds.), 117–28.

Gérin, D. 2009. "Sphinges perdues et retrouvées, cinq monnaies de Samothrace dans la collection Chandon de Briailles." In *KERMATIA PHILIAS, timētikos tomos gia ton Ioannē Toratosoglou*, ed. S. Drougou et al. Athens: 145–51.

Grandjean, C., and Moustaka, A., eds. 2013. *Aux origins de la monnaie fiduciaire: traditions métallurgiques et innovations numismatiques*. Bordeaux.

Hammond, N. G. L. 1997. "The lakes on the lower Strymon and Mt. Dionysos." *Ancient World* 28: 41–47.

Hansen, M. H. 2004. "Salamis." In *An Inventory of Archaic and Classical Poleis*, ed. M. H. Hansen and T. H. Nielsen. Oxford: 637–39.

Hardwick, N. 1993. "The coinage of Chios from the VIth to the IVth century BC." In *Actes du XIe Congrès International de Numismatique*, ed. T. Hackens and G. Moucharte. Louvain-la-Neuve: 211–22.

1996. "The solution to Thucydides VIII, 101.1: the 'Chian Fortieths.'" *Quaderni Ticinesi, Numismatica e Antichità Classiche* 25: 59–69.

1998. "The coinage of Terone from the fifth to the fourth centuries BC." In Ashton and Hurter (eds.), 119–34.

2010. "The Coinage of Chios 600–300 BC: new research developments 1991–2008." In *Coins in the Aegean Islands, Proceedings of the Fifth Scientific Meeting, Mytilene, 16–19 September 2006*, ed. P. Tselekas. *Obolos* 9, vol. I, 217–45.

Hardwick, N., Stos-Gale, Z. A., and Cowell, M. 1998. "Lead isotope analyses of Greek coins of Chios from the 6th – 4th centuries B.C." In *Metallurgy in Numismatics, Royal Numismatic Society Special Publication No. 4*, eds. A. Oddy and M. Cowell. London: 367–84.

Hitzl, K. 1996. *Die Gewichte Griechischer Zeit aus Olympia*. Olympische Forschungen 25. Berlin.

Howgego, C. 1990. "Why Did Ancient States Strike Coins?," *Numismatic Chronicle* 150: 1–25.

1995. *Ancient History from Coins*. London.

Kagan, J. H. 1987. "The decadrachm hoard: chronology and consequences." In Carradice (ed.), 21–8.

1998. "Epidamnus or Ephyre (Elea). A note on the coinage of Corinth and her colonies at the outbreak of the Peloponnesian War." In Ashton and Hurter (eds.), 163–73.

2008. "Paros, Melos and Naxos: archaic and early classical coinages of the Cyclades." *American Journal of Numismatics* 20: 105–11.

2013. "Epidamnus, Anactorium, and Potidaea: Corinthian-style Pegasi at the outbreak of the Peloponnesian War." *American Journal of Numismatics* 25: 1–9.

2014. "Notes on the coinage of Mende." *American Journal of Numismatics* 26: 1–32.

Kakavogiannis, E. 2001. "The silver ore processing workshops of the Lavrion region." *Annual of the British School at Athens* 96: 365–80.

2005. *Metalla ergasima kai synkechorēmmena: hē organōsē tēs ekmetalleusēs tou oryktou ploutou tēs Laureōtikēs apo tēn Athenaikē dēmokratia*. With English summary, 331–39, entitled "The organisation of the exploitation of the mineral wealth of Lavreotike by the Athenian democracy." Athens.

Kallet, L. 2001. *Money and the Corrosion of Power in Thucydides: The Sicilian Expedition and Its Aftermath.* Berkeley.

2004. "Epigraphic geography: the tribute quota fragments assigned to 421/0–415/4 B.C." *Hesperia* 73: 465–96.

2007. "The Athenian economy." In *The Cambridge Companion to the Age of Pericles*, ed. L. J. Samons II. Cambridge: 70–95.

Kallet-Marx, L. 1989. "The Kallias Decree, Thucydides, and the outbreak of the Peloponnesian War." *Classical Quarterly* 39: 94–113.

1993. *Money, Expense, and Naval Power in Thucydides' History 1-5.24.* Berkeley.

Karwiese, S. 1980. "Lysander as Herakliskos Drakonopnigon." *Numismatic Chronicle* 140: 1–27.

Konuk, K. 1998. "The early coinage of Kaunos." In Ashton and Hurter (eds.), 197–223.

2002. *Sylloge Nummorum Graecorum Turkey I: The Muharrem Kayhan Collection.* Istanbul.

2011. "Des chouettes en Asie Mineure: quelques pistes de réflexion." In Faucher, Marcellesi, and Picard (eds), 53–66.

Kraay, C. M. 1964. "The Melos hoard of 1907 re-examined." *Numismatic Chronicle and Journal of the Royal Numismatic Society* 54: 1–20.

1976. *Archaic and Classical Greek Coins.* London.

1979. "The coinage of Ambracia and the preliminaries of the Peloponnesian War." *Quaderni Ticinesi, Numismatica e Antichità Classiche* 8: 37–59.

Kraay, C. M., and Emeleus, V. M. 1962. *The Composition of Greek Silver Coins: Analysis by Neutron Activation.* Oxford.

Kroll, J. H. 1981. "From Wappenmünzen to gorgoneia to owls." *American Numismatic Society Museum Notes* 26: 1–32.

1993. *The Athenian Agora. Results of Excavations Conducted by the American School of Classical Studies in Athens*, vol. XXVI: *The Greek Coins.* Princeton.

1996. "The Piraeus 1902 hoard of plated drachms and tetradrachms." In *XAPAKTHP: Aphierōma stē Mandō Oikonomidou*, ed. E. Kypraiou. Athens: 139–46.

1998. Review of Hitzl (1996). *American Journal of Archaeology* 102: 632–33.

2001. "A small find of silver bullion from Egypt." *American Journal of Numismatics* 13: 1–20.

2008. "The monetary use of weighed bullion in archaic Greece." In *The Monetary Systems of the Greeks and Romans*, ed. W. V. Harris. Oxford: 12–37.

2009. "What about coinage?" In *Interpreting the Athenian Empire*, eds. J. Ma, N. Papazarkadas, and R. Parker. London: 195–209.

2011a. "The reminting of Athenian silver coinage, 353 BC." *Hesperia* 80: 229–56.

2011b. "Athenian tetradrachm coinage of the first half of the fourth century BC." *Revue Belge de Numismatique* 157: 3–26.

2013. "Salamis Again." In Grandjean and Moustaka (eds.), 109–16.

2015. "Small bronze tokens from the Athenian Agora, *symbola or kollyboi?*" In Wartenberg and Amandry (eds.), 107–16.

2017. "Striking and restriking on folded flans: evidence from Athens, Cyzicus, (?)Sinope, Elis, Thebes, and Aegina." In *Proceedings of the XV International Numismatic Congress, Taormina, September 21–25, 2015*, ed. M. Caltabiano. Rome-Messina 378–82.

2018. "Two lead weights of Kyzikos on the fifth-century commercial standard of Athens." In Tekin (ed.), 85–90.

2020. "Reconstructing the chronology of Athenian balance weights on the 'Solonian' trade standard." In *Pondera Antiqua et Mediaevalia* I, (Numismatica Lovaniensia 22), eds. C. Doyen and L. Willocx. Louvain-la-Neuve: 47–69.

Lang, M., and Crosby, M. 1964. *The Athenian Agora. Results of Excavations Conducted by the American School of Classical Studies in Athens, vol. X: Weights, Measures and Tokens.* Princeton.

Lawton, C. L. 1995. *Attic Document Reliefs.* Oxford.

Le Rider, G. 2001. *La naissance de la monnaie: pratiques monétaires de l'Orient ancient.* Paris.

Liampi, K. 2005. *Argilos: A Historical and Numismatic Study.* Athens.

Loomis, W. 1992. *The Spartan War Fund: IG V 1, 1 and a New Fragment.* Stuttgart.

Mackil, E., and Van Alfen, P. G. 2006. "Cooperative Coinage." In *Agoranomia: Studies in Money and Exchange Presented to John H. Kroll*, ed. P. G. Van Alfen. New York: 201–46.

Marcellesi, M.-C. 2000. "Commerce, monnaies locales et monnaies communes." *Revue des études grecques.* 113: 326–58.

Martin, T. R. 1985. *Sovereignty and Coinage in Classical Greece.* Princeton.

Matthaiou, A. P. 2009. *Studies in Attic Inscriptions and the History of the Fifth Century B.C.* PhD thesis, La Trobe University, Australia.

May, J. M. F. 1950. *Ainos, Its History and Coinage, 474–341 B.C.* Oxford.

Meadows, A. 2009. "Money in an ideal World: Plato's Laws and the Dual nature of Coinage." In *KERMATIA PHILIAS, timētikos tomos gia ton Ioannē Toratosoglou*, ed S. Drougou et al. Athens: 24–31.

2011a. "The Chian revolution: changing patterns of hoarding in 4th-century BC Western Asia Minor." In Faucher, Marcellesi, and Picard (eds.), 273–95.

2011b. "Athenian coin dies from Egypt: the new discovery at Heracleion." *Revue Belge de Numismatique* 157: 95–116.

2014. "The spread of coins in the Hellenistic World." In *Explaining Monetary and Financial Innovation: A Historical Analysis*, ed. P. Bernholz and R. Vaubel. Berlin: 169–94.

Meiggs, R. 1972. *The Athenian Empire.* Oxford.

Melville Jones, J. R. 1998. "The Value of Electrum in Greece and Asia." In Ashton and Hurter (eds.), 259–68.

Mørkholm, O. 1982. "Some reflections on the production and use of coinage in ancient Greece." *Historia* 31: 290–305.

Nicolet-Pierre, H. 1996. "Or Perse en Grèce: deux trésors de dariques conservés à Athènes." In *XAPAKTHP: Aphierōma stē Mandō Oikonomidou*, ed. E. Kypraiou. Athens: 200–08.

1998. "Autour de décadrachme athenien conservé à Paris." In Ashton and Hurter (eds.), 293–99.

Nixon, L., and Price, S. 1990. "The size and resources of Greek cities." In *The Greek City from Homer to Alexander*, ed. O. Murray and S. Price. Oxford: 137–70.

Nollé, J., and Wenninger, A. 1998/1999. "Themistokes und Archepolis: Eine griechische Dynastie im Perserreich und ihre Münzprägung." *Jahrbuch für Numismatik und Geldgeschichte* 47: 29–70 (with English summary).

Osborne, R. 1999. "Archaeology and the Athenian empire." *Transactions and Proceedings of the American Philological Association* 129: 319–32.

Picard, O. 1978. "La tortue de terre sur les monnaies d'Egine." *Bulletin de la Société fraçaise de numismatique* 33: 330–33.

2011. "La circulation monétaire dans le monde grec: le cas de Thasos." In Faucher, Marcellesi, and Picard (eds.), 79–109.

Pines, Y. et al., eds. 2014. *Birth of an Empire: The State of Qin Revisited*. Berkeley.

Pointing, M., Gitler, H., and Tal, O. 2011. "Who minted those owls? Metallurgical analyses of Athenian-styled tetradrachms found in Israel." *Revue Belge de Numismatique* 157: 117–32.

Price, M. J., and Waggoner, N. M. 1975. *Archaic Greek Coinage: The Asyut Hoard*. London.

Psoma, S. 2001. *Olynthe et les Chalcidiens de Thrace: études de numismatique et d'histoire*. Stuttgart.

2008. *The Coins from Maroneia and the Classical City at Molyvoti: A Contribution to the History of Aegean Thrace*. Athens.

2011. "La circulation monétaire et la théaurisation en Thrace au Nord des Rhodopes." In Faucher, Marcellesi, and Picard (eds.), 143–68.

2015a. "Did the so-called Thraco-Macedonian standard exist?" In Wartenberg and Amandry (eds.), 167–90.

2015b. "Athenian owls and the royal Macedonian monopoly on timber." *Mediterranean Historical Review* 30: 1–18.

Purcell, N. 2005. "The ancient Mediterranean: the view from the customs house." In *Rethinking the Mediterranean*, ed. W. V. Harris. Oxford: 200–32.

Raubitschek, A. 1941. "Two Notes on Isocrates." *Transactions and Proceedings of the American Philological Association* 72: 356–362.

Rhodes, P. J. 2008. "After the three-bar sigma controversy: the history of Athenian imperialism reassessed." *Classical Quarterly*, 2nd ser., 58: 500–06.

Rihll, T. E. 2001. "Making money in classical Athens." In *Economics Beyond Agriculture in the Classical World*, eds. D. J. Mattingly and J. Salmon. London: 115–42.

Robinson, E. S. G. 1947. 'The Tell El-Mashkuta hoard of Athenian tetradrachms."
    Numismatic Chronicle, 6th ser., 7: 115–21.
    1960. "Some problems in the later fifth century coinage of Athens." *American
    Numismatic Society Museum Notes* 9: 1–15.
Rusten, J., ed. 2011. *The Birth of Comedy*. Baltimore.
Rutishauser, B. 2012. *Athens and the Cyclades: Economic Strategies*. Oxford.
Samons, L. J. II, 2000. *Empire of the Owl: Athenian Imperial Finance*. Stuttgart.
Seltman, C. 1933. *Greek Coins*. London.
Sheedy, K. A. 2006. *The Archaic and Early Classical Coinages of the Cyclades*. London.
    2012. "Aegina, the Cyclades, and Crete." In *The Oxford Handbook of Greek and
    Roman Coinage*, ed. W. E. Metcalf. Oxford: 105–28.
    2017. "Themistocles, his son Archepolis, and their successors (Themistocles V?):
    numismatic evidence for the rule of a dynasty at Magnesia on the Maeander."
    In *Text and the Material World: Essays in Honour of Graeme Clarke*, eds.
    E. Minchin and H. Jackson. Uppsala: 68–80.
Smith, D. R. 2005. "Evidence for the identification of Aphrodite on staters of
    Corinth." *Numismatic Chronicle* 165: 41–3.
Starr, C. G. 1970. *Athenian Coinage, 480–449 BC*. Oxford.
Stephanaki, V. E. 2012. *Kos* I. Rhodos.
Stephanakis, M. I., and Demetriou, E. 2015. *Ta nomismata tēs nēsou Rodou kata tēn
    archaiotēta: Ialysos, Lindos, Kamiros, Rodos*. Athens.
Stroud, R. S. 2006. *The Athenian Empire on Stone*. David M. Lewis Memorial
    Lecture, Oxford University. Published by the Greek Epigraphical Society,
    Athens.
Tal, O. 2012. "Greek coinages of Palestine." In *The Oxford Handbook of Greek and
    Roman Coinage*, ed. W. E. Metcalf. Oxford: 253–75.
Tekin, O., ed. 2018. *Proceedings of the Second International Congress on the History
    of Money and Numismatics in the Mediterranean World*. January 5–8, 2017.
    Antalya.
Thompson, W. E. 1964. "Gold and silver ratios at Athens during the fifth century."
    Numismatic Chronicle 7th ser., 4: 103–23.
    1966. "The Functions of the emergency coinages of the Peloponnesian War."
    Mnemosyne 4th ser., 19: 337–43.
    1970. "The gold Nikai and the coinage of Athens." *Numismatic Chronicle*, 7th
    ser., 10: 1–6.
Thonemann, P. 2015. *The Hellenistic World: Using Coins as Sources*. Cambridge.
Thür, G., and Faraguna, M. 2018. "Silver from Laureion: Mining, Smelting, and
    Minting." In *Infrastructure and Distribution in Ancient Economies, Proceed-
    ings of a conference held at the Austrian Academy of Sciences, October 28–31
    2014*, ed. B. Woytek. Vienna: 45–58.
Trundle, M. 2016. "Coinage and the economics of the Athenian empire." In *Circum
    Mare: Themes in Ancient Warfare*, ed. J. Armstrong. Leiden: 65–79.

Van Alfen, P. 2002. "The owls from the 1989 Syria hoard, with a review of pre-Macedonian coinage in Egypt." *American Journal of Numismatics* 14: 1–57.

2011. "Mechanisms for the imitation of Athenian coinage: Dekeleia and mercenaries reconsidered." *Revue Belge de Numismatique* 157: 55–93.

2016. "Aegean-Levantine trade, 600–300 BCE. Commodities, consumers and the problem of autarkeia." In *The Ancient Greek Economy. Markets, Households and City-states*, eds. E. M. Harris, D. M. Lewis, and M. Woolmer. Cambridge: 277–98.

Van Wees, H. 2013. *Ships and Silver, Taxes and Tribute: A Fiscal History of Archaic Athens.* London.

Warren, J. A. W. 2000. "The silver coins of Sikyon in Leiden: analyses and some comments on the coinage." In *Pour Denise, Diverissements Numismatiques*, eds. S. M. Hurter and C. Arnold-Biucchi. Bern: 201–10.

2009. "Sikyon: a case study in the adoption of a coinage by a polis in the fifth century BC." *Numismatic Chronicle* 169: 1–14.

Wartenberg, U. 2015. "Thraco-Macedonian bullion coinage in the fifth century B.C.: the case of Ichnai." In Wartenberg and Amandry (eds.), 347–64.

Wartenberg, U., and Amandry, M., eds. 2015. *ΚΑΙΡΟΣ: Contributions to Numismatics in Honor of Basil Demetriadi.* New York.

Weiser, W. 1989. "Die Eulen von Kyros dem Jüngeren: Zu den ersten Münzporträts lebender." *Zeitschrift für Papyrologie und Epigraphik* 76: 267–96.

Williams, C. 1986. "Corinth and the cult of Aphrodite." In *Corinthiaca: Studies in honor of Darrel A. Amyx*, ed. M. A. Del Chiaro. Columbia, Missouri: 12–24.

Index